Collins · *do brilliantly!*

ActiveRevision
KS3 Maths

■ **Kevin Evans**
■ **Keith Gordon**
■ Series editor: Jayne de Courcy

CONTENTS

INTRODUCTION: ABOUT THIS BOOK AND CD-ROM   4–5
TOUR OF THE CD-ROM   6–9

	Revise again	Revised & understood

NUMBER   **10–43**
BASIC NUMBER   **10–25**
  Place value   10
  Ordering decimals   12
  The four rules   14
  Long multiplication and division   16
  Adding and subtracting decimals   18
  Multiplying and dividing decimals   20
  Negative numbers   22
  Adding and subtracting negative numbers   24

FRACTIONS AND PERCENTAGES   **26–35**
  Simple fractions and percentages   26
  Cancelling fractions   28
  Fractions and decimals   30
  Calculating percentage parts   32
  Calculating one quantity as a percentage of another   34

RATIO AND FRACTIONS   **36–43**
  Ratio and direct proportion   36
  Calculating with ratios   38
  Adding fractions   40
  Multiplying and dividing fractions   42

ALGEBRA   **44–73**
NUMBER PATTERNS AND FORMULAE   **44–55**
  Recognising and describing number patterns   44
  Factors, multiples and square numbers   46
  Using letters to represent values   48
  Formulae expressed in words   50
  Formulae with two operations   52
  nth term of a sequence   54

COORDINATES AND GRAPHS   **56–63**
  Coordinates in the first quadrant   56
  Coordinates in all four quadrants   58
  Using coordinates for graphs   60
  Interpreting graphs   62

SOLVING EQUATIONS   **64–73**
  BODMAS and brackets   64
  Linear equations 1   66
  Linear equations 2   68
  Fractional equations   70
  Trial and improvement   72

CONTENTS

		Revise again	Revised & understood
SHAPE, SPACE AND MEASURES	**74–97**		
UNITS AND ANGLES	**74–83**		
Metric units	74		
Imperial units	76		
Measuring and drawing angles	78		
Angle facts	80		
Angles in parallel lines and polygons	82		
SHAPES AND NETS	84–91		
Symmetry	84		
Reflections and rotations	86		
Enlargements	88		
3-D shapes	90		
AREA AND VOLUME	**92–97**		
Perimeter and area	92		
Circumference and area of a circle	94		
Volume	96		
HANDLING DATA	**98–121**		
AVERAGES AND RANGE	98–105		
Frequency tables	98		
The median and the mean	100		
Grouped data and frequency diagrams	102		
Comparing distributions	104		
STATISTICAL REPRESENTATION	106–115		
Line graphs	106		
Pie charts	108		
Continuous data	110		
Scatter diagrams	112		
Surveys	114		
PROBABILITY	**116–121**		
Probability 1	116		
Probability 2	118		
Probability 3	120		
TEST PRACTICE: QUESTIONS	**122–136**		
Test Paper 1	122		
Test Paper 2	128		
Mental Mathematics Test	133		
TEST PRACTICE: ANSWERS	137–141		
Test Paper 1	137		
Test Paper 2	139		
Mental Mathematics Test	141		
INDEX	143		

ABOUT THIS BOOK AND CD-ROM

HOW *ACTIVE REVISION KS3 MATHS* WILL HELP YOU

Active Revision KS3 Maths is an entirely new **interactive** way to revise and boost your Test level. It will help you to prepare for your Test by:

- revising all the topics (**book**)
- testing you on your knowledge as you revise (**CD-ROM**)
- helping you approach Test questions with confidence (**book**)
- helping you plan your revision time effectively (**CD-ROM**)

WHAT THE BOOK CONTAINS

Key topics and worked examples
The content you need to revise is divided into twelve sections linked to the KS3 Maths Programme of Study. These sections are then sub-divided into a number of **two-page units**. You should be able to read through each unit in no more than 10–15 minutes. There are lots of **worked examples of Test questions (including Mental Test questions)** which will help you to apply your understanding.

Common Error
These boxes highlight the mistakes students most frequently make. By reading through these boxes carefully, you can ensure that you **avoid making these errors**.

Key Words and Tips
The Key Words boxes contain all the **mathematical terms** you **must** understand for your Test. The Tips boxes give you **extra help** with your revision.

UAM
Questions that test your ability to **use and apply** mathematics are highlighted. This type of question now appears in the National Tests.

Quick Check Tests and Final Tests
Each two-page unit has a linked Quick Check Test. Each of the twelve sections has a Final Test, which tests your understanding across all the units in that section. **Quick Check Tests and Final Tests are on the CD-ROM** (see pages 6–9).

Test practice
This section gives you practice at answering **Paper 1** and **Paper 2** Test questions. There is also a **Mental Test** for you to do.

HOW TO MAKE THE BEST USE OF THIS BOOK AND CD-ROM

Everyone has their own strengths and weaknesses, so the way in which you use **Active Revision KS3 Maths** is up to you. You can decide which of these approaches suits you better:

Option 1 – Revise steadily using the book and CD-ROM

1. One by one, complete each unit by **reading through the content** and then **doing the Quick Check Test** on the CD–ROM.

2. If you don't get full marks on the Quick Check Test, tick the **'revise again'** column on the contents list. This will help you keep track of the areas on which you need to spend more time.

3. If you do score full marks on the test, tick the **'revised and understood'** column on the contents list.

4. At the end of each section, complete the **Final Test** on the CD–ROM. This acts as a final check on understanding. The results of this appear automatically on your **personal Test Score Chart**. This will help you to **prioritise** the areas on which you need to spend further revision time.

Option 2 – Concentrate on your weak areas first

If you are short of time, you could opt for this approach to your Maths revision:

1. Do a number of **Quick Check Tests** on the CD-ROM in the areas where you think you are **weakest**.

2. If you don't score full marks on these tests, read through the units in the book.

3. If you have time, **try the Quick Check Tests for some of the areas you feel confident about too**, just to check you're not being overconfident!

4. Do all the **Final Tests** on the CD-ROM, as this will act as a double-check on your understanding. The results are automatically fed through to your **personal Test Score Chart**. This will help you to **prioritise** the areas you need to spend further time revising.

Remember, whichever option you choose, use the book and CD-ROM interactively to get instant feedback on your strengths and weaknesses.

HOW TO INSTALL YOUR CD-ROM

On most computers the Active Revision application will start automatically when you put the disc into the CD-ROM drive. If the application does not start automatically, you just need to double-click on the file on the CD-ROM called ar.exe (or ar.hqx if you're using a Mac).

> For minimum specifications to run the CD-ROM, see page 142.

If the application appears in a small window, you can hold down the CTRL key and press F to make it fill the whole screen.

1. WELCOME SCREEN

This is the first screen that you will see. Once the data has finished loading, click on the Continue button to get to the Main Menu.

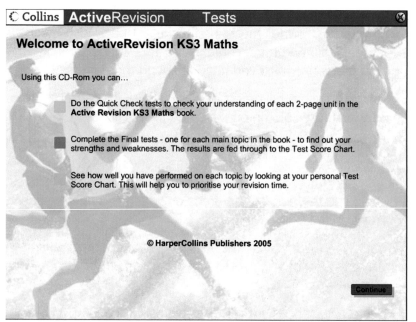

Welcome screen

2. MAIN MENU

This screen shows twelve topics, which correspond to the twelve main sections in the book. Click on Quick Check if you want to test your understanding of each unit in a topic. Click on Final Test if you want to test your understanding of a whole topic.

Main menu

3. THE QUICK CHECK TESTS

Selecting the test you want
Once you have selected your test topic, you will see all the unit tests listed for that topic. Just click on your selection!

Answering the questions
Each test consists of a number of short questions. Each question tells you exactly what you have to do.

If you want to redo a question before submitting your answer, click on the **Restart Question** button.

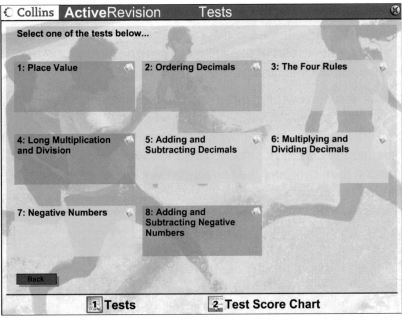

Test selection menu

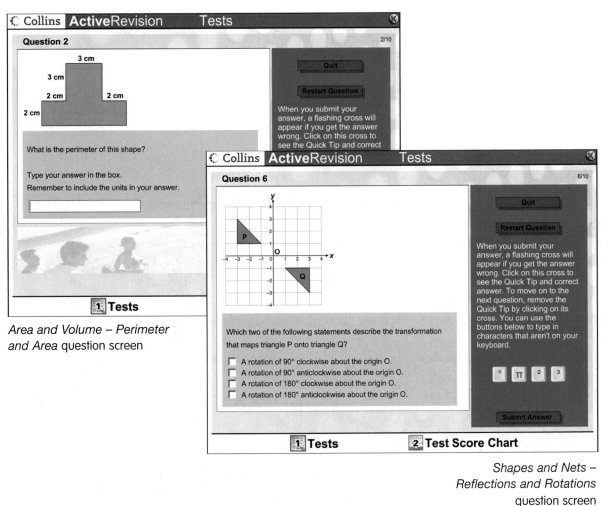

Area and Volume – Perimeter and Area question screen

Shapes and Nets – Reflections and Rotations question screen

Instant feedback

When you have completed a question, click on the **Submit Answer** button at the bottom of the screen or use the Enter key on your keyboard. If your answer is right, a red tick will appear.

If your answer is wrong, a red flashing cross will appear. Click on the cross and the correct answer will appear in the question window and the cross will change to a tick. A **Quick Tip** window will also appear, which will give you extra help or reiterate the correct answer. To close this window, click its small close button. You can then compare the correct answer with your own answer – just click on the red tick and your wrong answer will be displayed again. You can move backwards and forwards between the right answer and your wrong answer as many times as you like.

To go on to the next question, click on the **Next** button. Or, if you want to return to the unit selection menu, click on the **Quit** button. (Note: before you can move on, you must close the **Quick Tip** window.)

At the end of each test, your marks and score for that test will be displayed.

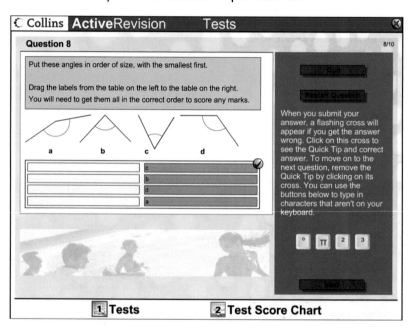

Units and Angles – Measuring and Drawing angles question screen

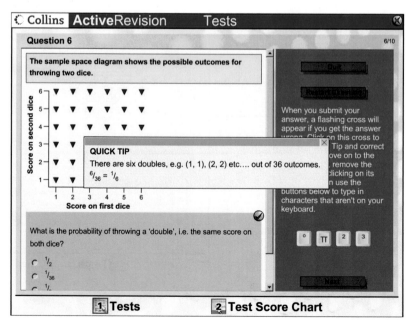

Probability – Probability 3 question screen

4. FINAL TESTS

You can go directly to these tests from the main menu. There is a Final Test for each of the twelve topics. The questions test your understanding across the whole of a topic. Your scores for each question are added together and then fed into your personal Test Score Chart (see below).

5. TEST SCORE CHART

Once you have completed all the questions in a Final Test, your marks are fed into the Test Score Chart so that you have a record of which tests you have completed and how well you have done. Your results are colour coded so you can see at a glance the areas in which you are weak. Remember, if you feel it will help, you can redo a test – perhaps after going back over the relevant unit in the book. The Test Score Chart will keep a record of your latest score only.

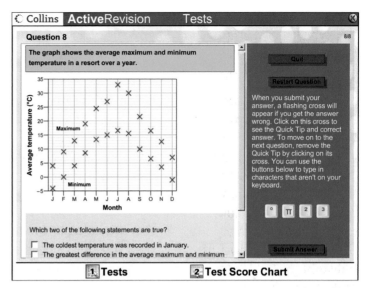

Final Test question

Topic Name	Max Score	Last Scored(%)	Attempts
Basic Number	11	81	1
Fractions and Percentages	8	25	1
Ratio and Fractions	8	25	1
Number Patterns and Formulae	test not attempted		
Coordinates and Graphs	7	14	1
Solving Equations	9	33	1
Units and Angles	test not attempted		
Shapes and Nets	test not attempted		
Area and Volume	8	25	1
Averages and Range	test not attempted		
Statistical Representation	test not attempted		
Probability	test not attempted		

Test Score Chart

PLACE VALUE

- You will already know about hundreds, tens and units.

  For example, in the number five hundred and eighty-three, there are:

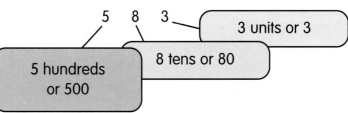

5   8   3

3 units or 3

8 tens or 80

5 hundreds or 500

- You may also know about the decimal point, which comes after the units and separates the whole numbers from the decimal fractions.

  For example, in the number 45.82, there are:

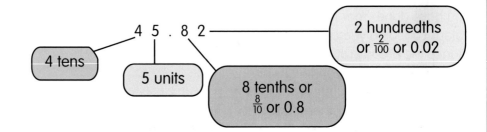

4 5 . 8 2

4 tens

5 units

8 tenths or $\frac{8}{10}$ or 0.8

2 hundredths or $\frac{2}{100}$ or 0.02

- When you multiply numbers by 10 or 100, the digits move one or two places to the left.

... TIP ...

- When you multiply a whole number by 10 or 100, you just add one or two zeros on the end. When you do this, you are actually moving the digits.

Example $34 \times 100 = 3400$

Th H T U
         3 4
3 4 0 0

COMMON ✗ ERROR

✗ $0.3 \times 100 = 0.300$

✓ You do not just add two zeros on the end. You need to move the digits:

$0.3 \times 100 = 30$

Example $46.23 \times 10 = 462.3$

H T U . $\frac{1}{10}$ $\frac{1}{100}$
      4 6 . 2   3
4 6 2 . 3

Example $0.4 \times 100 = 40$

T U . $\frac{1}{10}$
   0 . 4
4 0 .

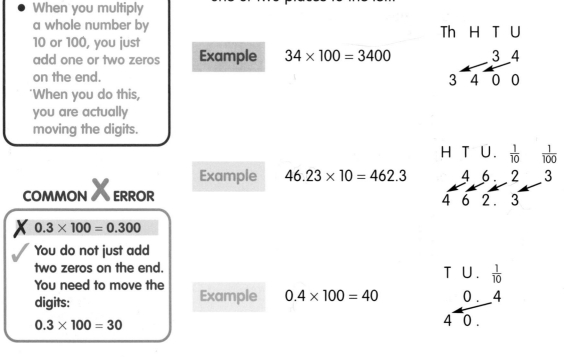

- National Test questions are straightforward, such as:

> **1** Work out
>
> **a** 100×43.2 **b** 3.45×10
>
> **c** 0.23×100 **d** 5.6×1000
>
> **ANSWERS**
>
> **1 a** 4320   **b** 34.5
>
>   **c** 23   **d** 5600

- Sometimes Test questions will test your understanding of place value.

> **2** Tracy has some number cards.
>
>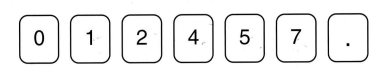
>
> **a** Make the largest three-digit odd number with three of the cards.
>
> **b** Tracy makes the number 52.7 with four of the cards. Use Tracy's cards to make a number that is **100 times** as big as 52.7.

ANSWERS

2 a

Pick the largest digit for the hundreds, then the next largest for the tens. Use 1 to make the number odd.

b

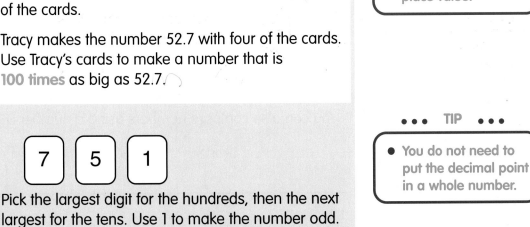

$52.7 \times 100 = 5270$

 Now try Basic Number Quick Check Test 1.

... TIP ...

- You can answer this type of question by moving the decimal point by 1, 2 or 3 places to the right.

  4 3 . 2 0

  3 . 4 5

  5 . 6 0 0

❓ UAM

- This is a Using and Applying maths question.

  You have to use your understanding of place value.

... TIP ...

- You do not need to put the decimal point in a whole number.

ORDERING DECIMALS

- thousandth
- greater than
- less than
- number line
- consecutive

- In the last section you met tenths and hundredths. The next place value to the right is thousandths. For example, in the number 3.529 there are:

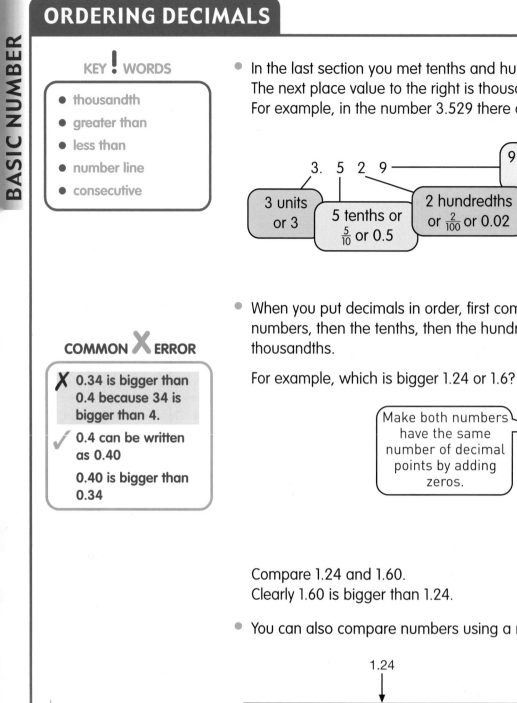

3. 5 2 9

3 units or 3

5 tenths or $\frac{5}{10}$ or 0.5

2 hundredths or $\frac{2}{100}$ or 0.02

9 thousandths or $\frac{9}{1000}$ or 0.009

- When you put decimals in order, first compare the whole numbers, then the tenths, then the hundredths and then the thousandths.

For example, which is bigger 1.24 or 1.6?

Make both numbers have the same number of decimal points by adding zeros.

COMMON X ERROR

X 0.34 is bigger than 0.4 because 34 is bigger than 4.

✓ 0.4 can be written as 0.40

0.40 is bigger than 0.34

Compare 1.24 and 1.60.
Clearly 1.60 is bigger than 1.24.

- You can also compare numbers using a number line.

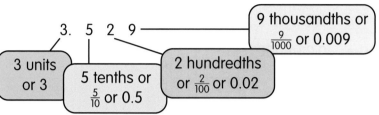

1.24

1.6

1.0   1.1   1.2   1.3   1.4   1.5   1.6   1.7

Numbers on the right are bigger.

• • • TIP • • •

- 'Is bigger than' can be shown by this symbol: >

● National Test questions are straightforward, such as:

1   This is part of a number line.

   a   Fill in the three missing numbers.

| 5.4 | 5.5 | 5.6 | 5.7 | 5.8 | ...... | ...... | ...... |

   b   Complete this sentence:

   The numbers go up in steps of …

ANSWERS

1   a   5.9, 6.0, 6.1

   b   0.1
   Any 'step' is the difference between two consecutive numbers.

••• TIP •••

● You can write 6.0 as 6 as it is a whole number.

COMMON ✗ ERROR

✗ Writing 6.0 as 5.10 because the series is 5.7, 5.8, 5.9, …

✓ The '10' is actually a whole unit:

$5.0 + 1.0 = 6.0$

2   Freddy, Mary and Alice are members of a family.
Freddy is 1.36 metres tall.
Mary is 1.5 metres tall.
Alice is 0.98 metres tall.

   a   Put the children in order of size with the smallest first.

   b   Another child, Ben, is 0.5 metres shorter than Freddy.
   How tall is Ben?

ANSWERS

2   a   Write all the heights with the same number of decimal places.
   Freddy 1.36, Mary 1.50, Alice 0.98
   So the order of size is: Alice, Freddy, Mary.

   b $1.36 - 0.5 = 0.86$

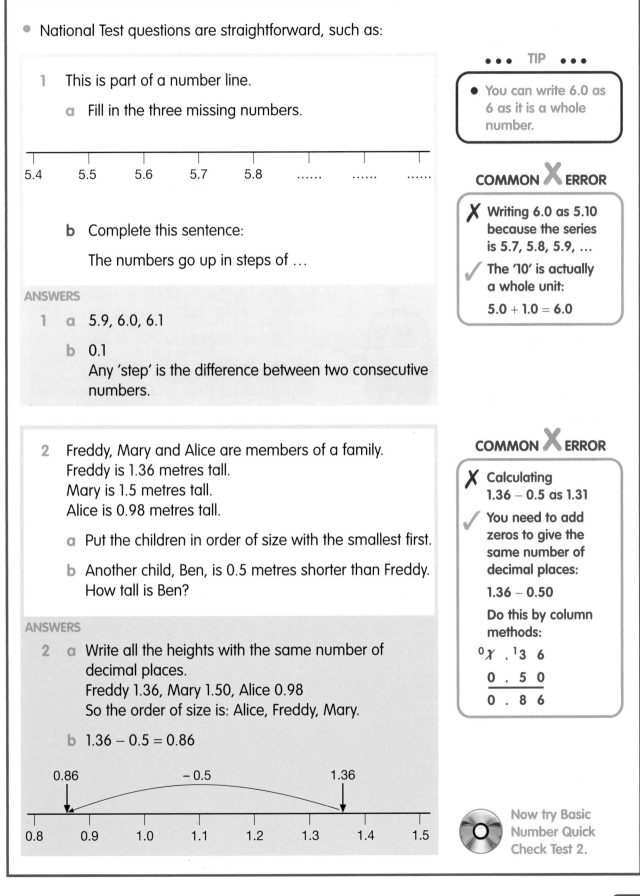

COMMON ✗ ERROR

✗ Calculating $1.36 - 0.5$ as 1.31

✓ You need to add zeros to give the same number of decimal places:

$1.36 - 0.50$

Do this by column methods:

```
 0    1
 ✗ . 3 6
 0 . 5 0
─────────
 0 . 8 6
```

Now try Basic Number Quick Check Test 2.

THE FOUR RULES

KEY **!** WORDS

- tables
- addition
- subtraction
- multiplication
- division
- sum
- product
- difference

... TIP ...

- The 1, 2, 5 and 10 times table are fairly easy to remember. The 9 times table can be done using your fingers,

  e.g. 4×9

  Hold your hands up and fold down the fourth finger:

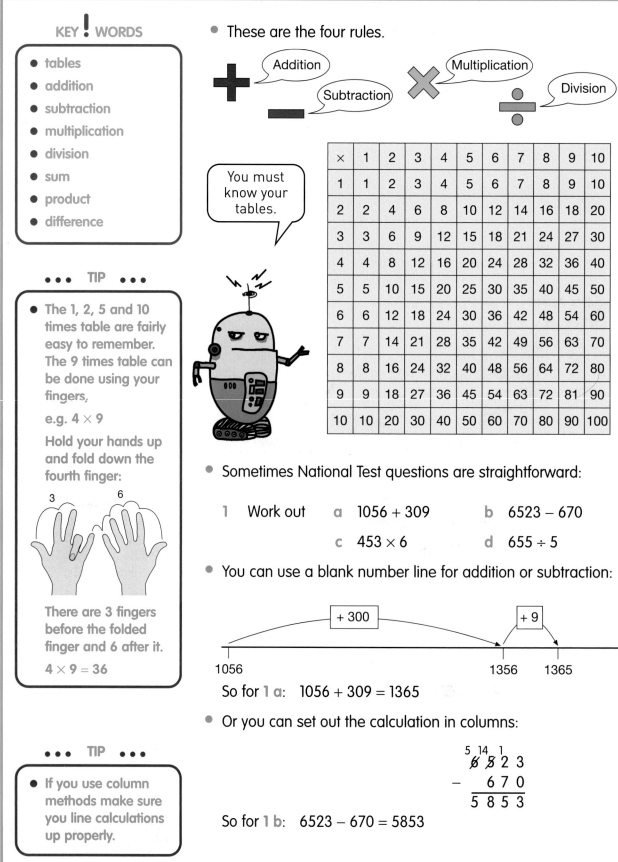

  There are 3 fingers before the folded finger and 6 after it.

  $4 \times 9 = 36$

... TIP ...

- If you use column methods make sure you line calculations up properly.

- These are the four rules.

  Addition

  Subtraction

  Multiplication

  Division

  You must know your tables.

×	1	2	3	4	5	6	7	8	9	10
1	1	2	3	4	5	6	7	8	9	10
2	2	4	6	8	10	12	14	16	18	20
3	3	6	9	12	15	18	21	24	27	30
4	4	8	12	16	20	24	28	32	36	40
5	5	10	15	20	25	30	35	40	45	50
6	6	12	18	24	30	36	42	48	54	60
7	7	14	21	28	35	42	49	56	63	70
8	8	16	24	32	40	48	56	64	72	80
9	9	18	27	36	45	54	63	72	81	90
10	10	20	30	40	50	60	70	80	90	100

- Sometimes National Test questions are straightforward:

  1   Work out   **a** $1056 + 309$ **b** $6523 - 670$

  c 453×6 **d** $655 \div 5$

- You can use a blank number line for addition or subtraction:

  $+ 300$ $+ 9$

  1056   1356   1365

  So for **1 a**: $1056 + 309 = 1365$

- Or you can set out the calculation in columns:

  $$\begin{array}{r} {}^{5}\,{}^{14}\,{}^{1}\!\!\!\not{6}\,\not{5}\,2\,3 \\ -\quad 6\,7\,0 \\ \hline 5\,8\,5\,3 \end{array}$$

  So for **1 b**: $6523 - 670 = 5853$

You can do short multiplication or division in columns:

$$
\begin{array}{r}
4\ 5\ 3 \\
\times \qquad 6 \\
\hline
2\ 7\ 1\ 8 \\
3\ \ 1 \quad
\end{array}
$$

TIP

- Show the carry and borrowing digits.

So for **1 c**: $453 \times 6 = 2718$

Or you can do it in 'bits':

$$
\begin{array}{r}
600 \div 5 = 120 \\
50 \div 5 = \ \ 10 \\
5 \div 5 = \ \ \ \underline{1} \\
131
\end{array}
$$

So for **1 d**: $655 \div 5 = 131$

Sometimes questions expect you to work out what is required:

---

2   Look at the sign for a car park.

How much does it cost to park for an hour?

> **Car Park**
> **35p for 15 minutes**

? UAM

- This is a Using and Applying maths question.

  You need to realise how many lots of 15 minutes there are in an hour.

ANSWER

2   There are lots of ways to do these calculations but always show your method.

There are 4 lots of 15 minutes in one hour so the calculation is 4×35.

$4 \times 30 = 120$

$\underline{4 \times 5 = \ \ 20}$

$4 \times 35 = 140$

So it costs 140p or £1.40 to park for one hour.

Now try Basic Number Quick Check Test 3.

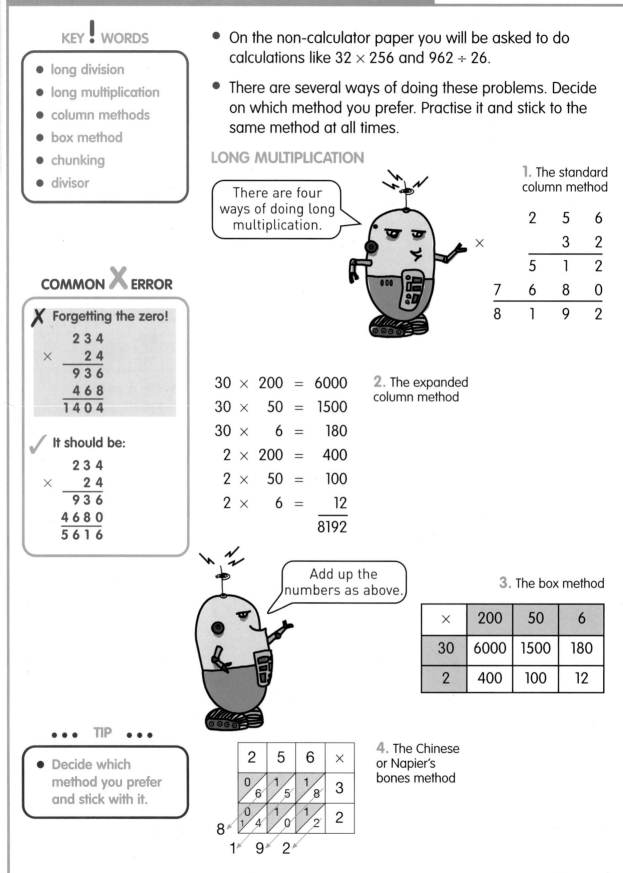

KEY **!** WORDS

- long division
- long multiplication
- column methods
- box method
- chunking
- divisor

- On the non-calculator paper you will be asked to do calculations like 32×256 and $962 \div 26$.

- There are several ways of doing these problems. Decide on which method you prefer. Practise it and stick to the same method at all times.

LONG MULTIPLICATION

There are four ways of doing long multiplication.

COMMON **X** ERROR

X Forgetting the zero!

```
    2 3 4
  ×   2 4
    9 3 6
    4 6 8
  1 4 0 4
```

✓ It should be:

```
    2 3 4
  ×   2 4
    9 3 6
  4 6 8 0
  5 6 1 6
```

1. The standard column method

```
      2 5 6
  ×     3 2
      5 1 2
    7 6 8 0
    8 1 9 2
```

2. The expanded column method

$$30 \times 200 = 6000$$
$$30 \times 50 = 1500$$
$$30 \times 6 = 180$$
$$2 \times 200 = 400$$
$$2 \times 50 = 100$$
$$2 \times 6 = 12$$
$$\overline{8192}$$

Add up the numbers as above.

3. The box method

×	200	50	6
30	6000	1500	180
2	400	100	12

4. The Chinese or Napier's bones method

2	5	6	×
0/6	1/5	1/8	3
0/4	1/0	1/2	2

8 / 1 / 9 / 2

... TIP ...

- Decide which method you prefer and stick with it.

LONG DIVISION

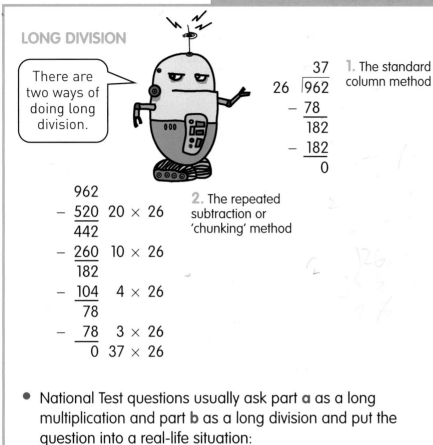

There are two ways of doing long division.

$$\begin{array}{r} 37 \\ 26\,\overline{)962} \\ -\,78 \\ \hline 182 \\ -\,182 \\ \hline 0 \end{array}$$

1. The standard column method

$$\begin{array}{r} 962 \\ -\,520 \quad 20 \times 26 \\ \hline 442 \\ -\,260 \quad 10 \times 26 \\ \hline 182 \\ -\,104 \quad 4 \times 26 \\ \hline 78 \\ -\,78 \quad 3 \times 26 \\ \hline 0 \quad 37 \times 26 \end{array}$$

2. The repeated subtraction or 'chunking' method

••• TIP •••

- Write out some of the easier times tables for the divisor:

$$1 \times 26 = 26$$
$$2 \times 26 = 52$$
$$4 \times 26 = 104$$
$$10 \times 26 = 260$$
$$20 \times 26 = 520$$

Subtract the biggest multiple you can each time.

••• TIP •••

- Estimate the answer as a check on your working:

$$28 \times 576p$$

Round this to
$$30 \times 600p$$
$$= 18\,000p$$
$$= £180$$

- National Test questions usually ask part **a** as a long multiplication and part **b** as a long division and put the question into a real-life situation:

> 1 **a** A garden centre has 576 winter pansies for sale.
> Each plant costs 28p.
> How much will all 576 cost?
>
>
>
> **b** The pansies are packed in trays of 18.
> How many trays does the garden centre have?

••• TIP •••

- Check an answer to a division by multiplying by the original divisor:

$$18 \times 32 =$$
$$10 \times 30 = 300$$
$$10 \times 2 = 20$$
$$8 \times 30 = 240$$
$$8 \times 2 = \underline{\quad 16}$$
$$576$$

ANSWERS

1 **a** This is done by the box method.
The total is £161.28.

×	500	70	6
20	10000	1400	120
8	4000	560	48

$$\begin{array}{r} 10000 \\ 1400 \\ 120 \\ 4000 \\ 560 \\ 48 \\ \hline 16128 \end{array}$$

b This is done by the standard method.
They have 32 trays.

$$\begin{array}{r} 32 \\ 18\,\overline{)576} \\ -\,540 \\ \hline 36 \\ -\,36 \\ \hline 0 \end{array}$$

Now try Basic Number Quick Check Test 4.

ADDING AND SUBTRACTING DECIMALS

- decimal point
- digit
- difference

- Adding and subtracting decimals is just like normal addition and subtraction. All you have to do is line up the decimal point.

Example   1.23 + 3.4

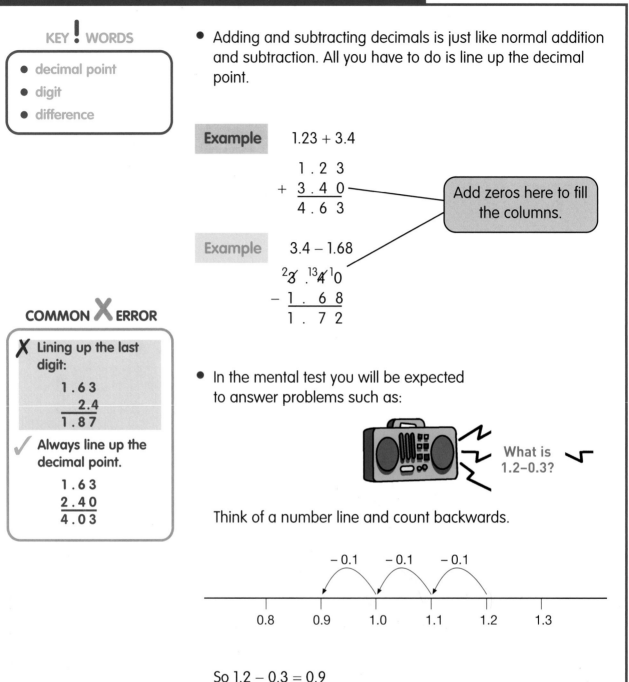

$$\begin{array}{r} 1.23 \\ +\ 3.40 \\ \hline 4.63 \end{array}$$

Add zeros here to fill the columns.

Example   3.4 − 1.68

$$\begin{array}{r} {}^2\cancel{3}.{}^{13}\cancel{4}\,{}^1 0 \\ -\ 1.68 \\ \hline 1.72 \end{array}$$

COMMON ✗ ERROR

✗ Lining up the last digit:

$$\begin{array}{r} 1.63 \\ 2.4 \\ \hline 1.87 \end{array}$$

✓ Always line up the decimal point.

$$\begin{array}{r} 1.63 \\ 2.40 \\ \hline 4.03 \end{array}$$

- In the mental test you will be expected to answer problems such as:

What is 1.2 − 0.3?

Think of a number line and count backwards.

So 1.2 − 0.3 = 0.9

- Additions and subtractions can also be done using a blank number line.

Example 1.36 + 2.75

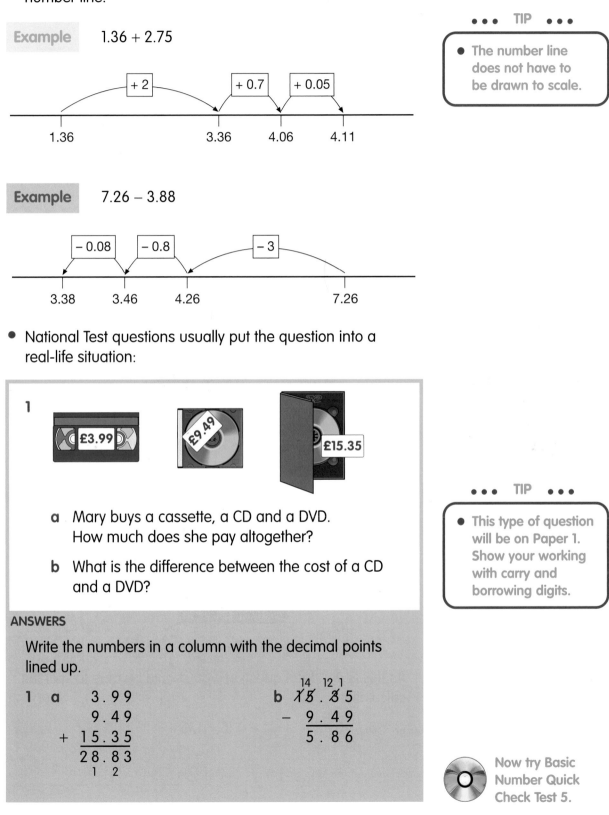

••• TIP •••

- The number line does not have to be drawn to scale.

Example 7.26 − 3.88

- National Test questions usually put the question into a real-life situation:

1

£3.99   £9.49   £15.35

a   Mary buys a cassette, a CD and a DVD. How much does she pay altogether?

b   What is the difference between the cost of a CD and a DVD?

••• TIP •••

- This type of question will be on Paper 1. Show your working with carry and borrowing digits.

ANSWERS

Write the numbers in a column with the decimal points lined up.

```
1  a     3.99                    b   14  12 1
         9.49                        1̶5̶ . 3̶ 5
     +  15.35                       −  9.49
        28.83                         5.86
         1  2
```

Now try Basic Number Quick Check Test 5.

MULTIPLYING AND DIVIDING DECIMALS

KEY ! WORDS

- decimal
- box method
- short division
- short multiplication

• • • TIP • • •

- Estimate the answer just to be sure:

  3.76×4 is approximately $4 \times 4 = 16$

  $8.04 \div 6$ is approximately $9 \div 6 = 1.5$

• • • TIP • • •

- 'Is approximately equal to' can be shown by this symbol: $\approx$

• • • TIP • • •

- In this type of question the numbers will be shown on the answer sheet to help you:

  3.45   3

• Multiplying and dividing decimals is just like normal multiplying and dividing. All you have to do is keep the decimal point lined up.

Example 3.76×4

$$
\begin{array}{r}
3\ .\ 7\ 6 \\
\times \qquad 4 \\
\hline
1\ 5\ .\ 0\ 4 \\
{\scriptstyle 1\ \ \ 3\ \ \ 2}
\end{array}
$$

Example $8.04 \div 6$

$$
\begin{array}{r}
1\ .\ 3\ 4 \\
6\ \overline{)8\ .\ ^2 0 ^2 4}
\end{array}
$$

The decimal point in the answer is underneath the point in the question.

• In the mental test you will be expected to solve problems such as:

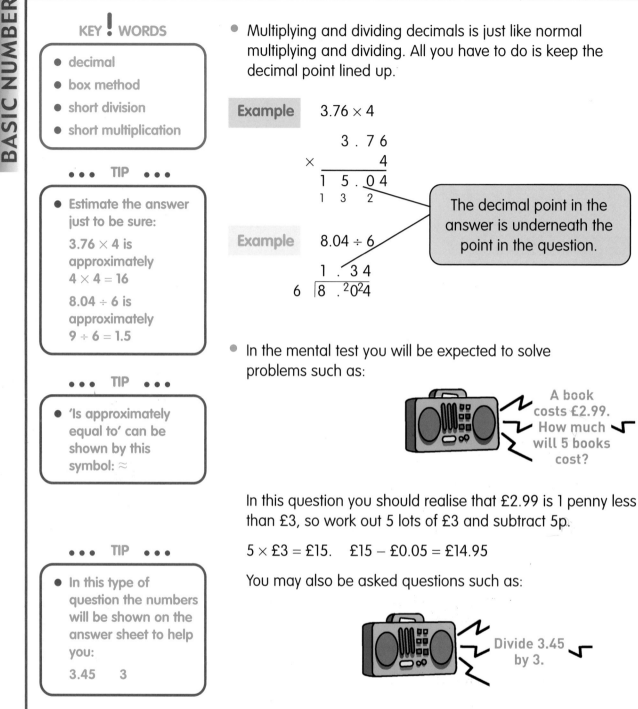

A book costs £2.99. How much will 5 books cost?

In this question you should realise that £2.99 is 1 penny less than £3, so work out 5 lots of £3 and subtract 5p.

$5 \times £3 = £15.$ $£15 - £0.05 = £14.95$

You may also be asked questions such as:

Divide 3.45 by 3.

As this is a mental question, you should be able to split the calculation:

$(3 \div 3) + (0.45 \div 3) = 1 + 0.15 = 1.15$

- National Test questions sometimes put the question into a real-life situation:

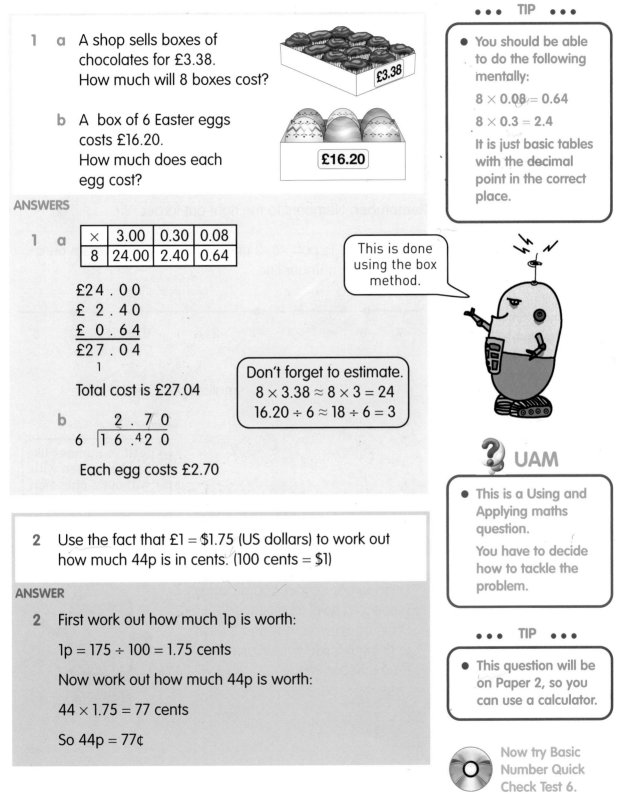

1 a A shop sells boxes of chocolates for £3.38.
How much will 8 boxes cost?

£3.38

   b A box of 6 Easter eggs costs £16.20.
How much does each egg cost?

£16.20

... TIP ...

- You should be able to do the following mentally:

$8 \times 0.08 = 0.64$

$8 \times 0.3 = 2.4$

It is just basic tables with the decimal point in the correct place.

ANSWERS

1 a

×	3.00	0.30	0.08
8	24.00	2.40	0.64

This is done using the box method.

£24 . 0 0
£ 2 . 4 0
£ 0 . 6 4
£27 . 0 4
      1

Total cost is £27.04

Don't forget to estimate.
$8 \times 3.38 \approx 8 \times 3 = 24$
$16.20 \div 6 \approx 18 \div 6 = 3$

   b
```
    2 . 7 0
6 |1 6 .⁴2 0
```

Each egg costs £2.70

? UAM

- This is a Using and Applying maths question.

You have to decide how to tackle the problem.

2 Use the fact that £1 = $1.75 (US dollars) to work out how much 44p is in cents. (100 cents = $1)

ANSWER

2 First work out how much 1p is worth:

1p = 175 ÷ 100 = 1.75 cents

Now work out how much 44p is worth:

$44 \times 1.75 = 77$ cents

So 44p = 77¢

... TIP ...

- This question will be on Paper 2, so you can use a calculator.

Now try Basic Number Quick Check Test 6.

KEY ! WORDS

- number line
- directed number
- negative
- positive

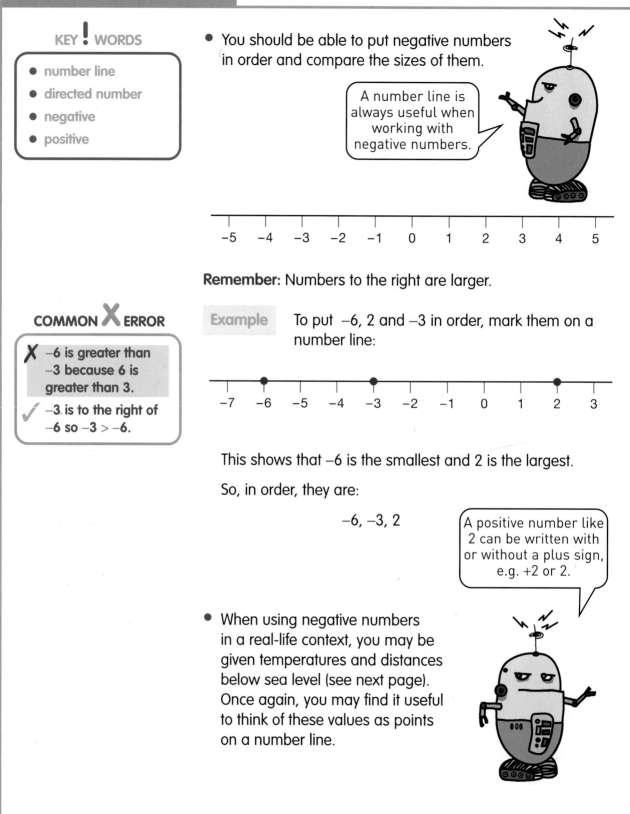

- You should be able to put negative numbers in order and compare the sizes of them.

A number line is always useful when working with negative numbers.

-5 -4 -3 -2 -1 0 1 2 3 4 5

Remember: Numbers to the right are larger.

COMMON X ERROR

X −6 is greater than −3 because 6 is greater than 3.

✓ −3 is to the right of −6 so −3 > −6.

Example To put −6, 2 and −3 in order, mark them on a number line:

-7 -6 -5 -4 -3 -2 -1 0 1 2 3

This shows that −6 is the smallest and 2 is the largest.

So, in order, they are:

−6, −3, 2

A positive number like 2 can be written with or without a plus sign, e.g. +2 or 2.

- When using negative numbers in a real-life context, you may be given temperatures and distances below sea level (see next page). Once again, you may find it useful to think of these values as points on a number line.

● Typical National Test questions could be:

1 In Moscow, the temperature at midnight was −15 °C. At midday it was 2 °C.
What was the difference in temperature?

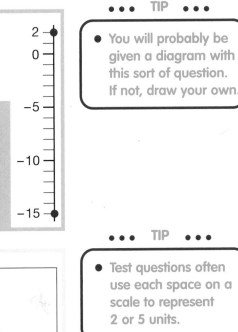

● ● ● TIP ● ● ●

● You will probably be given a diagram with this sort of question. If not, draw your own.

ANSWERS

1 If these two values are plotted on a vertical number line, you can see the difference is 17 °C.

Alternatively, it is 15 °C below zero and 2 °C above, giving a difference of 17 °C.

● ● ● TIP ● ● ●

● Test questions often use each space on a scale to represent 2 or 5 units.

2 A skyscraper has 8 floors below ground and 62 floors above ground.

A lift is at the 6th floor below ground (−6) and then rises 42 floors. How many floors above ground will it be when it stops?

ANSWERS

2 6 floors will take it to ground level. This leaves 36 floors to go, so the lift will stop at the 36th floor above ground.

This is the same problem as −6 + 42, which is covered in the next unit.

3 A thermometer shows the following two temperatures at 6.00 am and 4.00 pm.

What is the difference in temperature?

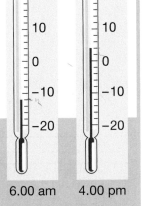

6.00 am   4.00 pm

ANSWERS

3 The two temperatures are −12 °C and 4 °C.

The difference is 16 °C.

COMMON ✘ ERROR

✘ **Misreading scales**
✓ **Always look at the scale and decide what each space is worth. In this case each space is worth 2 degrees.**

Now try Basic Number Quick Check Test 7.

KEY ! WORDS

- negative
- positive
- directed numbers

... TIP ...

- Negative and positive numbers are sometimes called directed numbers, because they can have a direction on a number line. Negative numbers go to the left (or down) and positive numbers go to the right (or up).

COMMON ✗ ERROR

✗ Taking two minus signs together as a minus:
$6 - -5 = 6 - 5 = 1$

✓ The correct answer is $6 - -5 = 6 + 5 = 11$.

... TIP ...

- When you add a negative number, it is the same as subtracting a positive number.

- You need to be able to add and subtract positive and negative numbers. A number line can be useful.

Always start at zero. Count to the left for negative numbers and to the right for positive numbers.

Example   Work out $+5 - 7$.

Starting at zero, first move 5 units to the right and then move 7 units to the left.

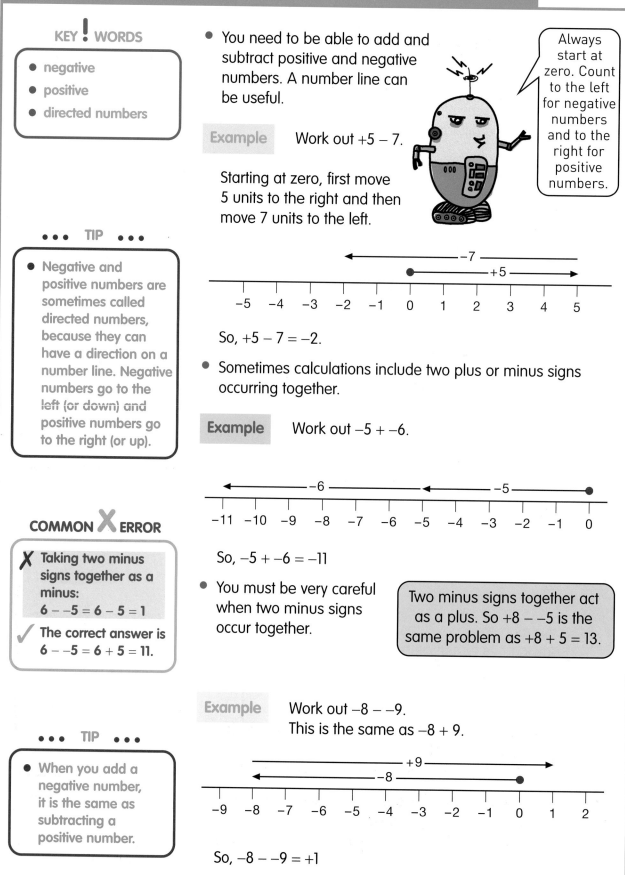

So, $+5 - 7 = -2$.

- Sometimes calculations include two plus or minus signs occurring together.

Example   Work out $-5 + -6$.

So, $-5 + -6 = -11$

- You must be very careful when two minus signs occur together.

Two minus signs together act as a plus. So $+8 - -5$ is the same problem as $+8 + 5 = 13$.

Example   Work out $-8 - -9$.
This is the same as $-8 + 9$.

So, $-8 - -9 = +1$

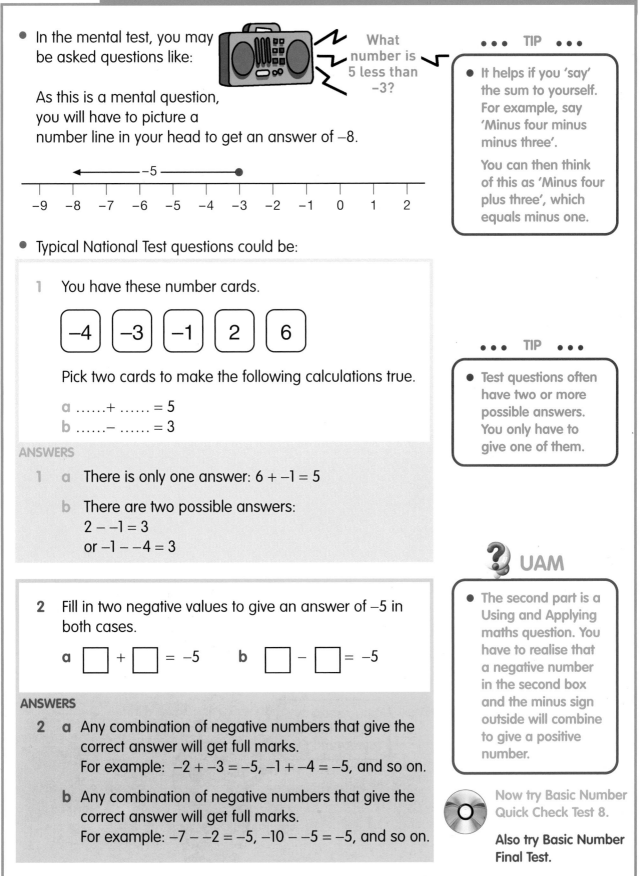

- In the mental test, you may be asked questions like:

  What number is 5 less than −3?

  As this is a mental question, you will have to picture a number line in your head to get an answer of −8.

••• TIP •••

- It helps if you 'say' the sum to yourself. For example, say 'Minus four minus minus three'.

  You can then think of this as 'Minus four plus three', which equals minus one.

- Typical National Test questions could be:

  1   You have these number cards.

  -4 -3 -1 2 6

  Pick two cards to make the following calculations true.

  a …… + …… = 5
  b …… − …… = 3

••• TIP •••

- Test questions often have two or more possible answers. You only have to give one of them.

ANSWERS

1   a   There is only one answer: $6 + -1 = 5$

    b   There are two possible answers:
        $2 - -1 = 3$
        or $-1 - -4 = 3$

? UAM

- The second part is a Using and Applying maths question. You have to realise that a negative number in the second box and the minus sign outside will combine to give a positive number.

2   Fill in two negative values to give an answer of −5 in both cases.

    a   ☐ + ☐ = −5   b   ☐ − ☐ = −5

ANSWERS

2   a   Any combination of negative numbers that give the correct answer will get full marks.
        For example: $-2 + -3 = -5$, $-1 + -4 = -5$, and so on.

    b   Any combination of negative numbers that give the correct answer will get full marks.
        For example: $-7 - -2 = -5$, $-10 - -5 = -5$, and so on.

Now try Basic Number Quick Check Test 8.

Also try Basic Number Final Test.

SIMPLE FRACTIONS AND PERCENTAGES

- You need to be able to recognise some simple fractions and percentages.

For example, in this pie chart what fraction is blue?
Half ($\frac{1}{2}$) of the pie is labelled blue.

What percentage is red?
A quarter is labelled red, so the percentage is 25%.

Favourite colours

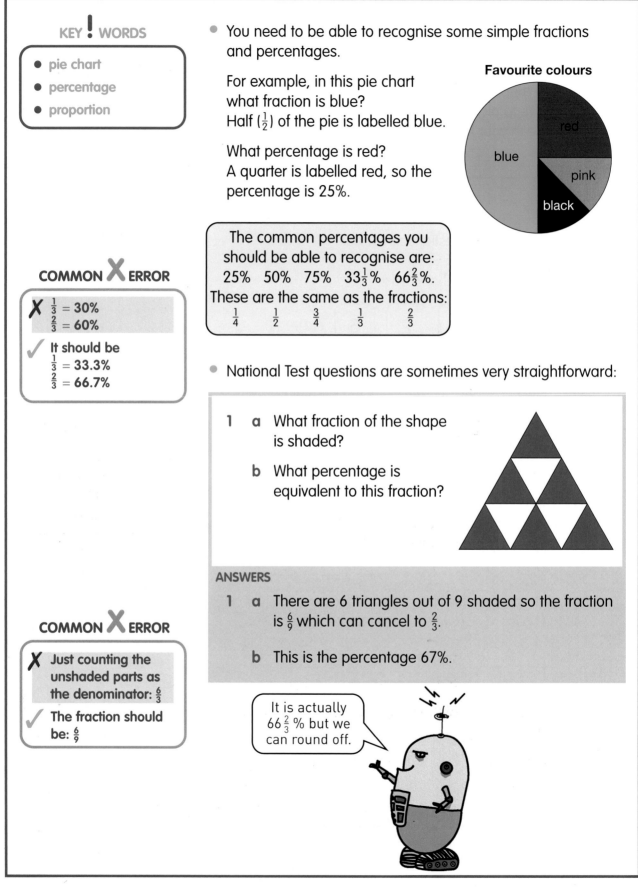

COMMON ✗ ERROR

✗ $\frac{1}{3}$ = 30%
$\frac{2}{3}$ = 60%

✓ **It should be**
$\frac{1}{3}$ = 33.3%
$\frac{2}{3}$ = 66.7%

The common percentages you should be able to recognise are:
25% 50% 75% 33$\frac{1}{3}$% 66$\frac{2}{3}$%.
These are the same as the fractions:
$\frac{1}{4}$ $\frac{1}{2}$ $\frac{3}{4}$ $\frac{1}{3}$ $\frac{2}{3}$

- National Test questions are sometimes very straightforward:

1 a What fraction of the shape is shaded?

b What percentage is equivalent to this fraction?

ANSWERS

1 a There are 6 triangles out of 9 shaded so the fraction is $\frac{6}{9}$ which can cancel to $\frac{2}{3}$.

b This is the percentage 67%.

COMMON ✗ ERROR

✗ Just counting the unshaded parts as the denominator: $\frac{6}{3}$

✓ The fraction should be: $\frac{6}{9}$

It is actually 66$\frac{2}{3}$% but we can round off.

● Sometimes questions can be more complicated, such as:

2 The pie charts show the ages of people in a village and a town.

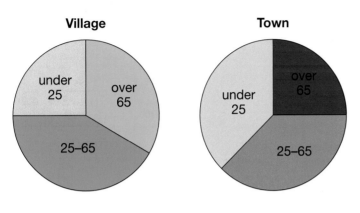

Village   **Town**

a What percentage of the village are over 65?

b What percentage of the town are over 65?

c Tick the box that is true.

☐ There are more people over 65 in the village than the town.

☐ There are fewer people over 65 in the village than the town.

☐ There are equal numbers of people over 65 in the village than the town.

☐ You cannot tell how many people over 65 there are in the village and the town.

Explain your answer.

ANSWERS

2 a There are 33% of the people in the village over 65.

b There are 25% of the people in the town over 65.

c You cannot tell how many people are over 65 because the pie chart only shows the proportions and not the actual numbers. There may be more people in the town so 25% of a larger population may be more than 33% of a smaller population.

 UAM

● This question wants you to realise that the area of the pie chart only represents the *proportion of the data* and not the *actual number*.

COMMON ✗ ERROR

✗ 33% of one pie chart represents more than 25% of another.

✓ Pie charts only compare proportions and do not tell you actual values.

●●● TIP ●●●

● A third is actually $33\frac{1}{3}$% but we can round off.

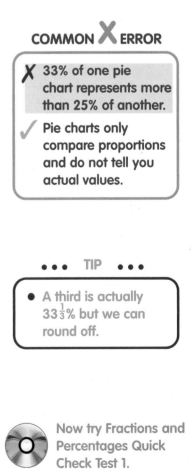

Now try Fractions and Percentages Quick Check Test 1.

CANCELLING FRACTIONS

- cancelling
- simplest from
- lowest terms
- numerator
- denominator
- equivalent

- Cancelling fractions means looking for a common factor on the top and bottom. Once this is cancelled, the fraction is in its 'simplest form' or 'lowest terms'.

Example The fraction $\frac{15}{20}$ can be cancelled by a common factor of 5 to $\frac{3}{4}$:

Cancelling means divide the top number (numerator) and the bottom number (denominator) by the common factor.

$$\frac{15 \div 5}{20 \div 5} = \frac{3}{4}$$

We usually just write this as

$$\frac{\cancel{15}^{\,3}}{\cancel{20}_{\,4}}$$

••• TIP •••

- Look for the largest number that divides into both the numerator and the denominator.

- To find an equivalent fraction, you can multiply the numerator and denominator by the same number.

Example

$$\frac{3}{5} = \frac{12}{20} \quad \text{because} \quad \frac{3 \times 4}{5 \times 4} = \frac{12}{20}$$

- In the mental test, you may be asked a question such as:

Look at the fraction $\frac{4}{12}$. Write it in its simplest form.

The common factor is 4, so divide top and bottom by 4 to give the answer of $\frac{1}{3}$.

- Other mental test questions may be of the form:

Multiply the top and bottom by the same number:

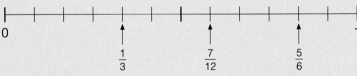

$$\frac{2 \times 2}{3 \times 2} = \frac{4}{6} \qquad \frac{2 \times 6}{3 \times 6} = \frac{12}{18} \qquad \frac{2 \times 10}{3 \times 10} = \frac{20}{30}$$

Circle all the fractions equivalent to $\frac{2}{3}$.

$\frac{12}{18}$ $\frac{4}{5}$ $\frac{4}{6}$ $\frac{20}{30}$ $\frac{4}{9}$

- National Test questions usually ask you to fill in a numerator or denominator when you are given the other one.

1   Look at the fractions $\frac{1}{3}$, $\frac{7}{12}$, $\frac{5}{6}$.

  a   Mark each fraction on the number line.
      The first one is done for you.

0                     $\frac{1}{3}$ 1

  b   Fill in the missing numbers.

$$\frac{3}{4} = \frac{\square}{20} \qquad \frac{1}{3} = \frac{9}{\square} \qquad \frac{5}{\square} = \frac{6}{24}$$

••• TIP •••

- Count the divisions, in this case 12, as this will help you to place the fractions.

  The number of divisions will always be a multiple of the numerators of the fractions.

ANSWERS

1   a   There are 12 divisions, so each space is $\frac{1}{12}$.
        $\frac{5}{6}$ is $\frac{10}{12}$.

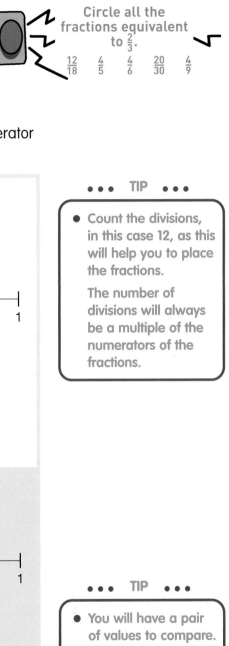

0                 $\frac{1}{3}$ $\frac{7}{12}$ $\frac{5}{6}$ 1

••• TIP •••

- You will have a pair of values to compare. If the denominators are 4 and 20, the multiplier will be 5.

  b   Decide what number the given values are multiplied by and do the same to the other one.

  The multipliers in the first two parts are 5 and 9.
  In the third part the cancelled fraction is $\frac{1}{4}$, so the values are divided by 6 and then multiplied by 5.

$$\frac{3}{4} = \frac{\boxed{15}}{20} \qquad \frac{1}{3} = \frac{9}{\boxed{27}} \qquad \frac{5}{\boxed{20}} = \frac{6}{24}$$

Now try Fractions and Percentages Quick Check Test 2.

FRACTIONS AND DECIMALS

KEY ! WORDS

- equivalent
- percentages
- fractions
- decimals

- Fractions, percentages and decimals represent the same value and you should know the equivalences between them.

- You should know the following equivalences:

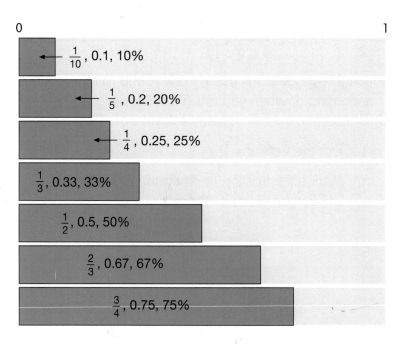

0   1

$\frac{1}{10}$, 0.1, 10%

$\frac{1}{5}$, 0.2, 20%

$\frac{1}{4}$, 0.25, 25%

$\frac{1}{3}$, 0.33, 33%

$\frac{1}{2}$, 0.5, 50%

$\frac{2}{3}$, 0.67, 67%

$\frac{3}{4}$, 0.75, 75%

COMMON ✗ ERROR

✗ Because $10\% = \frac{1}{10}$, so $5\% = \frac{1}{5}$.

✓ However, $5\% = \frac{1}{20}$ and $20\% = \frac{1}{5}$.

- If you know the equivalences above, you can use them to work out others:

Example
$$40\% = 2 \times 20\% = 2 \times \frac{1}{5} = \frac{2}{5}$$
$$= 2 \times 0.2 = 0.4$$
$$= 2 \times 20\% = 40\%$$

- In the mental test, you may be asked questions such as:

COMMON ✗ ERROR

✗ $2 \times \frac{1}{5} = \frac{2}{10}$ i.e. both top and bottom are multiplied by 2.

✓ Only the numerator is multiplied by 2.

The correct answer is $2 \times \frac{1}{5} = \frac{2}{5}$

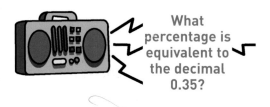

What percentage is equivalent to the decimal 0.35?

As this is a mental question, you should be able to split the calculation:

$$0.35 = 3 \times 0.1 + 0.05 = 30\% + 5\% = 35\%$$

- In the mental test, you may also be asked:

What fraction is equivalent to the decimal 0.6?

••• TIP •••

- $0.6 = 0.1 \times 6$ so you could write $\frac{6}{10}$, as this is an equivalent fraction.

As this is a mental question, you should be able to split the calculation:

$0.6 = 3 \times 0.2 = 3 \times \frac{1}{5} = \frac{3}{5}$

- National Test questions usually ask you to estimate fractions or percentages of shapes:

---

1 About 40% of this shape is shaded grey.

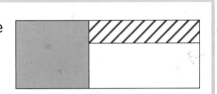

a Approximately what percentage is striped?

b Approximately what percentage is white?

ANSWERS

1 a The remaining area is 60%.
About one third of this is striped.
One third of 60% is 20%.

b This has to be your answer to part **a** subtracted from 60%.
$60\% - 20\% = 40\%$

••• TIP •••

- An answer of 18%–22% would be acceptable, but it is best to give a rounded answer.

••• TIP •••

- Remember to count all triangles, shaded and unshaded, to find the denominator.

---

2 Look at the diagram.

a What fraction is shaded?

b What percentage is shaded?

ANSWERS

2 a The fraction is $\frac{8}{20}$ which can be cancelled to $\frac{2}{5}$.

b $\frac{2}{5}$ as a percentage is $2 \times \frac{1}{5} = 2 \times 20\% = 40\%$.

••• TIP •••

- 4 is the largest number that divides into both 8 and 20.

 Now try Fractions and Percentages Quick Check Test 3.

FRACTIONS AND PERCENTAGES

KEY ! WORDS

- percentage part
- increase
- decrease
- multiplier

- You should know that per cent means 'out of a hundred'.

- There are two types of percentage question you may be asked. The first is working out a percentage of a quantity. On the non-calculator paper, the percentage will always be a multiple of 5 or 10.

Example   Work out 15% of £45.

10% of £45 is £4.50, so 5% of £45 is £2.25

So 15% of £45 is £4.50 + £2.25 = £6.75

Example   Work out 32% of 75 kg.

On your calculator, find $32 \div 100 \times 75 = 24$ kg

or $0.32 \times 75 = 24$ kg.

- In the mental test you may be asked questions like:

What is 20% of £30?

As this is a mental question, start by calculating 10%, which is £3, and then double it to give £6.

- You may also be asked to increase or decrease a quantity by a certain percentage.

Example   A car's top speed is 125 mph. After a tune-up, its top speed increases by 12%. What is the new top speed?

There are two ways to do this.

Method 1

Work out 12% of 125.

$12 \div 100 \times 125 = 15$

Add this to the original speed: 125 + 15 = 140 mph.

... TIP ...

- On the non-calculator paper, always start with 10% of a quantity. The percentage required will then be a multiple of this or involve 5%, which is half of this quantity.

... TIP ...

- Think of the per cent sign as '÷ 100' and the 'of' as a multiplication sign. So 43% of 150 is $43 \div 100 \times 150 = 64.5$.

Method 2

Use a multiplier. A 12% increase is a multiplier of 1.12.
$1.12 \times 125 = 140$ mph

- Typical National Test questions could be:

---

1 This is how Mary works out $12\frac{1}{2}$% of £56.

10% of £56 $= £5.60$ (so, 5% of £56 $= £2.80$)

$2\frac{1}{2}\%$ of £56 $= \underline{£1.40}$

$12\frac{1}{2}\%$ of £56 $= £7.00$

> If you know that the equivalent fraction to $12\frac{1}{2}$%
> is $\frac{1}{8}$, you could do this as £56 ÷ 8 = £7.

Use Mary's method or one of your own to work out
$17\frac{1}{2}$% of £36.

ANSWER

1 10% of £36 $= £3.60$

5% of £36 $= £1.80$

$2\frac{1}{2}\%$ of £36 $= £0.90$

$17\frac{1}{2}\%$ of £36 $= \underline{£6.30}$

---

2 Phil has 60 female budgies.

30% of them lay two eggs and the rest lay one egg.

How many eggs were laid?

ANSWER

2 30% of 60 $= 3 \times 10\% = 3 \times 6 = 18$ budgies

18 budgies lay 2 eggs $= 36$ eggs

Total eggs $= 36 + 42 = 78$ eggs

> 30% is a multiplier of 0.3, so $60 \times 0.3 = 18$.

• • • TIP • • •

- Calculations are much easier if you use a multiplier.

  32% is a multiplier of 0.32.

  An increase of 15% is a multiplier of 1.15.

  A decrease of 8% is a multiplier of 0.92

  You can easily convert percentages to decimals. Just divide by 100 (or move digits).

• • • TIP • • •

- $17\frac{1}{2}$% is the current VAT rate, so this is a special percentage and is likely to be used in questions.

  If you have this on a calculator paper, use a multiplier of 1.175.

 UAM

- Here you have to work out the different number of budgies.

  It is important in this type of question that you show all your working. You can still gain marks even if you make the odd mistake.

Now try Fractions and Percentages Quick Check Test 4.

FRACTIONS AND PERCENTAGES

KEY **!** WORDS

- percentage
- out of

• • • TIP • • •

- Think of 'out of' as divide, so 42 out of 56 means 42 ÷ 56.

• • • TIP • • •

- If you divide the numerator by the denominator, this gives the percentage multiplier: 42 ÷ 56 = 0.75, which is 75%.

COMMON **✗** ERROR

✗ Calculating the percentage that 32 is out of 40 as 32 × 40 ÷ 100.

✓ It should be: 32 × 100 ÷ 40 (= 80%)

- You may be asked to work out one quantity as a percentage of another.

> A key phrase in this type of question is 'out of'.

Example   What percentage is 42 out of 56?

The fraction is $\frac{42}{56}$.
This is divided to give the decimal,
$42 \div 56 = 0.75$.
This decimal is multiplied by 100 to give the percentage.
The whole calculation can be done as
$42 \div 56 \times 100 = 75\%$

- On the non-calculator paper, the fractions will cancel to common fractions such as $\frac{1}{10}$, $\frac{1}{5}$ and $\frac{1}{4}$.

- You should know the equivalent percentages to these, or multiply top and bottom to make the denominator 100.

Example   17 pupils in a class of 25 stay for school dinners. What percentage is this?

The fraction is $\frac{17}{25}$.

Multiply the numerator (top number) and the denominator (bottom number) by 4.

$$\frac{17 \times 4}{25 \times 4} = \frac{68}{100}$$

So the answer is 68%.

- In the mental test, you may be asked questions like:

> In a test I got 16 out of 20. What percentage did I get?

Convert the denominator to 10 or 100.

So 16 out of 20 is the same as 8 out of 10, which is 80%.

• Typical National Test questions could be:

---

1 What percentage of each diagram is shaded?

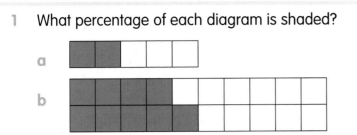

a

b

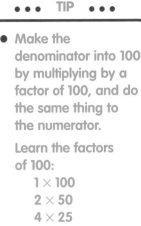

• Make the denominator into 100 by multiplying by a factor of 100, and do the same thing to the numerator.

Learn the factors of 100:

1×100
2×50
4×25
5×20
10×10

ANSWERS

1 a There are 2 squares out of 5 shaded.

This is $\frac{2}{5}$ or $\frac{40}{100}$ (multiply top and bottom by 20), so 40% is shaded.

b There are 9 squares out of 20 shaded.

This is $\frac{9}{20}$ or $\frac{45}{100}$ (multiply top and bottom by 5), so 45% is shaded.

---

2 30 pupils were asked how they travelled to school.

	Boys	Girls
Walk	2	6
Bus	1	9
Car	2	7
Cycle	0	3
Total	5	25

a What percentage of boys come by bus?

b What percentage of girls walk to school?

c Stanley said 'Girls are healthier than boys because more of them walk to school'. Explain why Stanley was wrong.

 UAM

• This is a Using and Applying maths question. You have to realise that even though more girls than boys walk, as a proportion there are more boys than girls.

ANSWERS

2 a 1 out of 5 is 20%.

b 6 out of 25 is $\frac{6}{25} = \frac{24}{100} = 24\%$.

> You should know that $\frac{1}{5} = 20\%$.

c Although more girls than boys walk (6 compared to 2), the percentages are $\frac{2}{5} = 40\%$ for boys, and $\frac{6}{25} = 24\%$ for girls.

Now try Fractions and Percentages Quick Check Test 5.

Also try Fractions and Percentages Final Test.

KEY ! WORDS

- ratio
- simplest form
- unitary method

• Ratio is a way of comparing quantities.

• For example, if there are 18 girls and 12 boys in a class, the ratio is 18 : 12.

• Because 18 and 12 have a common factor of 6, this can be cancelled down to 3 : 2. This is called the simplest form.

Example   Reduce the ratio 15 : 25 to its simplest form.

The highest common factor of 15 and 25 is 5.
Cancelling (dividing) both numbers by 5 gives 3 : 5.

• You may also be asked direct proportion questions such as:

Example   If 6 pencils cost £1.32, how much will 10 pencils cost?

You can answer this in two ways:

• Using **ratio**
6 : 132 cancels to 1 : 22
So, multiplying by 10 gives 10 : 220, so 10 pencils will cost £2.20.

• Using the **unitary method**
If 6 pencils cost £1.32, 1 pencil costs $1.32 \div 6 = £0.22$
So 10 pencils cost $10 \times £0.22 = £2.20$

••• TIP •••

- Use whichever method is easiest for the question. The unitary method is easier for this example because 6 : 132 is not an easy ratio to cancel.

These two methods are basically the same.

• In the mental test, you may be asked questions like:

Look at the ratio 4 : 10. Write it in its simplest form.

The numbers will make finding a common factor easy.

In this case they cancel by 2 to give 2 : 5.

● Typical National Test questions could be:

---

1 To make green paint, 2 parts of yellow paint are mixed with 3 parts of blue paint.

   a How much of each type of paint will you need to make 10 litres of green paint?

   b To make dark green paint, John mixes 2 litres of yellow with 8 litres of blue.
      Write this ratio in its simplest form.

ANSWERS

1 a The ratio 2 : 3 has 5 parts, so to make 10 litres you will need 4 litres of yellow and 6 litres of blue.

   b The ratio for dark green is 2 : 8.
      This cancels by 2 to give 1 : 4.

---

2 Ernie is 4 years old. His brother Eric is 10 years old.

   a Write the ratio of Ernie's age to Eric's age as a ratio in its simplest form.

   b When Ernie is 10 years old, write the ratio of Ernie's age to Eric's age as a ratio in its simplest form.

ANSWERS

2 a The ratio is 4 : 10 which cancels to 2 : 5.

   b When Ernie is 10, Eric will be 16 so the ratio is 10 : 16 which cancels to 5 : 8.

---

3 5 chocolate bars cost £1.75.

   How much will 8 bars cost?

ANSWER

3 1 bar costs £1.75 ÷ 5 = £0.35

   8 bars cost 8 × £0.35 = £2.80

● ● ● **TIP** ● ● ●

● Check that your answers add up to the correct amount:
4 litres plus 6 litres = 10 litres.

 **UAM**

● Part (b) is a Using and Applying maths question. You have to remember to work out the new ages for both children.

● ● ● **TIP** ● ● ●

● This question would be on Paper 2 so you will be able to use a calculator.

You could use ratios:
   5 : 175
   1 : 35
   8 : 280

 Now try Ratio and Fractions Quick Check Test 1.

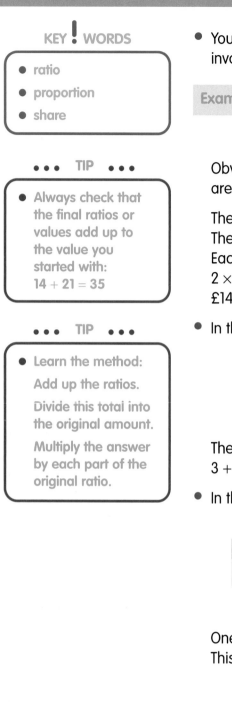

KEY ! WORDS

- ratio
- proportion
- share

• • • TIP • • •

- Always check that the final ratios or values add up to the value you started with:
  $14 + 21 = 35$

• • • TIP • • •

- Learn the method:

  Add up the ratios.

  Divide this total into the original amount.

  Multiply the answer by each part of the original ratio.

- You need to be able to carry out different calculations involving ratios.

  Example   If a family of 3 and a family of 2 had a meal and decided to split the bill of £35 between the two families, what should each family pay?

Obviously it would not be fair to split the bill in two, as there are more people in one of the families.

The bill should be split in the ratio $2 : 3$.
The ratio $2 : 3$ is a total of $2 + 3 = 5$ shares.
Each share will be $35 \div 5 = 7$.
$2 \times 7 = 14$ and $3 \times 7 = 21$, so the £35 should be split as £14 and £21.

- In the mental test, you may be asked questions like:

Divide £100 in the ratio $3 : 7$.

The numbers will be easy to divide.
$3 + 7 = 10$, $100 \div 10 = 10$, so the shares are £30 and £70.

- In the mental test, you may also be asked questions such as:

A fruit drink has orange and grapefruit juice mixed in the ratio $3 : 1$. How much orange juice should I use to make a litre of the drink?

One litre is 1000 ml, so divide 1000 in the ratio $3 : 1$.
This gives $750 : 250$, so 750 ml of orange is needed.

● Typical National Test questions could be:

1 Shade the diagram so that the ratio of shaded squares to unshaded squares is 3 : 5.

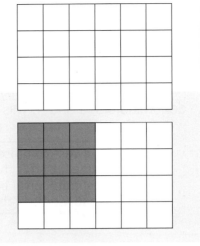

ANSWER

1 There are 24 squares, so divide 24 in the ratio 3 : 5. This gives 9 : 15.

So 9 squares should be shaded.

 UAM

● Part (b) of this question is Using and Applying maths.

You need to remember that the ages have all increased by one year.

2 Aunt Vera decides to give her nephews, Arnie, Barney and Clyde, £180. The money is to be divided in the ratio of their ages.

Arnie is 1, Barney is 2 and Clyde is 3.

a How much do they each receive?

b The next year she decides to share another £180 between the three boys in the ratio of their ages.

How much do they each receive the following year?

ANSWERS

2 a The total of their ages is 6, so divide 180 by 6.
180 ÷ 6 = 30, so

Arnie gets 1 × 30 = £30,
Barney gets 2 × 30 = £60,
and Clyde gets 3 × 30 = £90

b The following year the ages are 2, 3 and 4.
This is a total of 9.   180 ÷ 9 = 20, so

Arnie gets 2 × 20 = £40,
Barney gets 3 × 20 = £60,
and Clyde gets 4 × 20 = £80

●●● **TIP** ●●●

● Don't forget to check the totals:
30 + 60 + 90 = 180
40 + 60 + 80 = 180

 Now try Ratio and Fractions Quick Check Test 2.

ADDING FRACTIONS

COMMON ✗ ERROR

✗ $\frac{1}{2} + \frac{1}{3} = \frac{2}{5}$,

that is, the numerators are added and the denominators are added.

✓ The denominators must be the same and then only the numerators are added.

$\frac{1}{2} + \frac{1}{3} = \frac{3}{6} + \frac{2}{6}$

$= \frac{5}{6}$

••• TIP •••

- Some rulers marked like this

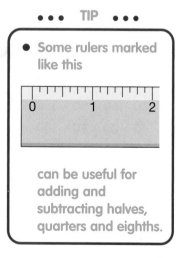

can be useful for adding and subtracting halves, quarters and eighths.

- You can only add and subtract fractions if they have the same denominator.

Example   Add $\frac{2}{3} + \frac{1}{4}$.

First, find the lowest common multiple of the two denominators, 3 and 4. This is 12.

> The lowest common multiple (LCM) is the smallest number in both the 3 and 4 times table.

Now make both fractions into twelfths.

$\frac{2}{3} = \frac{8}{12}$ (Multiply both top and bottom by 4)

$\frac{1}{4} = \frac{3}{12}$ (Multiply both top and bottom by 3)

Then just add the numerators and leave the denominator unchanged.

$$\frac{2}{3} + \frac{1}{4} = \frac{8}{12} + \frac{3}{12} = \frac{11}{12}$$

> A fraction like $\frac{17}{12}$ is called **top heavy**. It can be made into the mixed number $1\frac{5}{12}$.

- In the mental test, you may be asked questions such as:

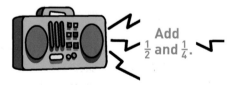

Add $\frac{1}{2}$ and $\frac{1}{4}$.

The fractions will be really easy, so you should know that $\frac{1}{2} + \frac{1}{4} = \frac{3}{4}$.

- Sometimes National Test questions are straightforward:

---

1 Add $\frac{3}{10}$ and $\frac{2}{5}$.

ANSWER

1 The common denominator is 10.

The first fraction is already in tenths.

$\frac{2}{5} = \frac{4}{10}$ (Multiply top and bottom by 2)

The calculation is $\frac{3}{10} + \frac{4}{10} = \frac{7}{10}$

Sometimes the questions are in a context:

---

2 A vegetable plot is planted with beans, peas, cabbages and carrots.

The peas take up $\frac{1}{4}$ of the plot.

The beans take up $\frac{3}{8}$ of the plot.

The cabbages take up $\frac{1}{6}$ of the plot.

How much of the plot is planted with carrots?

ANSWER

2 The total planted with peas, beans and cabbage is

$$\frac{1}{4} + \frac{3}{8} + \frac{1}{6}$$

The common denominator is 24.
Making all the fractions into fractions with a denominator of 24 gives

$$\frac{6}{24} + \frac{9}{24} + \frac{4}{24} = \frac{19}{24}$$

So $1 - \frac{19}{24} = \frac{5}{24}$ is planted with carrots.

··· **TIP** ···

- Subtracting is the same process as adding but the numerators are subtracted:

$$\frac{1}{2} - \frac{1}{3} = \frac{3}{6} - \frac{2}{6}$$
$$= \frac{1}{6}$$
$$\frac{7}{10} - \frac{2}{5} = \frac{7}{10} - \frac{4}{10}$$
$$= \frac{3}{10}$$

 UAM

- This is a Using and Applying maths question. You need to total the given fractions and then subtract this answer from 1.

··· **TIP** ···

- Subtracting a fraction from 1 is a common question:

$$1 - \frac{11}{14} = \frac{3}{14}$$
$$1 - \frac{7}{9} = \frac{2}{9}$$
$$1 - \frac{8}{11} = \frac{3}{11}$$

You should be able to see the relationship between the numerators and denominators.

 Now try Ratio and Fractions Quick Check Test 3.

MULTIPLYING AND DIVIDING FRACTIONS

- numerator
- denominator
- product
- simplest form

COMMON **✗** ERROR

✗ $\frac{1}{2} \times \frac{1}{2} = 1$

✓ The correct answer is
$\frac{1}{2} \times \frac{1}{2} = \frac{1}{4}$

• • • TIP • • •

- You can usually gain full marks on Test questions without cancelling but if the question says 'simplest form' then you must cancel down.

• • • TIP • • •

- $\frac{5}{2} = 5 \times \frac{1}{2}$
  $= 4 \times \frac{1}{2} + \frac{1}{2}$
  $= 2\frac{1}{2}$

  This is a mixed number.

- Adding and subtracting fractions requires denominators to be the same. Multiplying and dividing fractions is a little more straightforward.

Example   Multiply $\frac{2}{3} \times \frac{1}{4}$

When multiplying fractions, the new numerator is the product of the numerators and the new denominator is the product of the denominators.

Multiplying the numerators gives $2 \times 1 = 2$
Multiplying the denominators gives $3 \times 4 = 12$
So $\frac{2}{3} \times \frac{1}{4} = \frac{2}{12}$.
This fraction $\frac{2}{12}$ will cancel to $\frac{1}{6}$.

- To avoid problems with cancelling, cancel any fractions before multiplying.

$$\frac{{}^1\cancel{2}}{3} \times \frac{1}{\cancel{4}_2} = \frac{1}{6}$$

In this case, 2 on the top cancels with 4 on the bottom by a common factor of 2.

Example   Divide $\frac{5}{6} \div \frac{1}{3}$

When dividing fractions, turn the second fraction upside down and multiply.

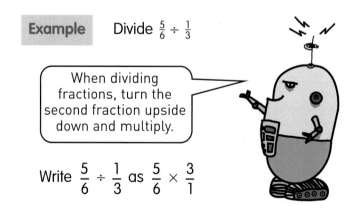

Write $\frac{5}{6} \div \frac{1}{3}$ as $\frac{5}{6} \times \frac{3}{1}$

Once again, cancel if you can. In this case 3 and 6 cancel by a common factor of 3.

$$\frac{5}{{}_2\cancel{6}} \times \frac{\cancel{3}^1}{1} = \frac{5}{2} = 2\frac{1}{2}$$

- In the mental test, you may be asked questions such as:

What is $\frac{1}{2}$ of $\frac{1}{3}$?

The fractions will be really easy, so you should know that
$\frac{1}{2} \times \frac{1}{3} = \frac{1}{6}$

- You may also be asked questions such as:

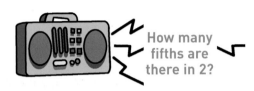

How many fifths are there in 2?

There are 5 fifths in 1, so there are 10 fifths in 2.

- National Test questions are usually straightforward:

---

1 Work out $3\frac{3}{4} \div \frac{5}{8}$

ANSWER

1 Write the calculation as $\frac{15}{4} \div \frac{5}{8}$

Now turn the second fraction upside down

and multiply $\dfrac{\overset{3}{\cancel{15}}}{\underset{1}{\cancel{4}}} \times \dfrac{\overset{2}{\cancel{8}}}{\underset{1}{\cancel{5}}} = \dfrac{6}{1}$

Cancel where possible.

The calculation is $3\frac{3}{4} \div \frac{5}{8} = 6$

••• TIP •••

- Always write mixed numbers as top heavy fractions when multiplying or dividing.
$3\frac{3}{4} = \frac{15}{4}$ because there are $3 \times 4 = 12$ quarters in 3 plus the extra 3 quarters.

••• TIP •••

- Any fraction with a denominator of 1 is a whole number.

Now try Ratio and Fractions Quick Check Test 4.

Also try Ratio and Fractions Final Test.

KEY WORDS

- sequence
- series
- term-to-term rule

••• TIP •••

- If you are asked to describe how a pattern builds up, say 'It goes up by 4 each time'.

••• TIP •••

- To spot a pattern, work out the differences:

```
  1    3    6    10    15
   \  / \  / \  /  \  /
    2    3    4    5
```

••• TIP •••

- A good way of remembering the triangle numbers is to think of snooker and ten-pin bowling. Snooker has 15 red balls in a triangle and ten-pin bowling has 10 pins in a triangle.

- A number pattern is a sequence or series of numbers that follow a rule.

- You should be able to say what are the next two terms in this sequence:

$$3, 7, 11, 15, 19, ..., ...$$

First look for the rule.

In this case each number is 4 more than the previous number.

This is called the **term-to-term rule**.

So the next two numbers are $19 + 4 = 23$ and $23 + 4 = 27$.

- Sometimes the term-to-term rule is not so straightforward:

Example Find the next two terms in this series of numbers and describe how the series is developed:

$$1, 3, 6, 10, 15, ..., ...$$

The next two terms are 21 and 28.

The series is building up by adding on 2, 3, 4, etc.

> The series 1, 3, 6, 10, 15, ... is a special series called the triangle numbers because the numbers can be made into triangle patterns.
>
> ° °° °°° °°°° °°°°°

- In the mental test, you may be asked questions like:

I start at 5 and count down in equal steps: 5, 2, −1. What is the next number in the sequence?

••• TIP •••

- Mental questions like this usually have the numbers written on the answer sheet to help you:

    5, 2, −1, …

Use these to decide on the term-to-term rule.

First decide on the step, which in this case, is subtract 3. Minus 1 subtract 3 is minus 4, so the answer is −4.

- National Test questions often involve a diagram:

1   The diagrams show some patterns made with triangular tiles.

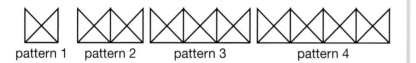

pattern 1   pattern 2   pattern 3   pattern 4

••• TIP •••

- It is always worth writing the number pattern out:

    3, 6, 9, 12, …

to help you find the term-to-term rule.

   a   Each pattern adds more tiles.
       How many more tiles are added each time?

   b   How many tiles will be needed for Pattern 6?

   c   60 tiles are used to make a pattern.
       What is the pattern number?

ANSWERS

1   a   3 more tiles are added each time.

   b   Adding three tiles on twice more gives:

$$12 + 3 = 15$$
$$15 + 3 = 18$$

So 18 tiles are used for pattern 6.

   c   You should see that the pattern is the 3-times table:

        3, 6, 9, 12, …

So for 60 tiles, $60 \div 3 = 20$, and the pattern number is 20.

Now try Number Patterns and Formulae Quick check Test 1.

FACTORS, MULTIPLES AND SQUARE NUMBERS

KEY ! WORDS

- factor
- multiple
- square number
- prime number

• • • TIP • • •

- Factors come in pairs except for square numbers, where one number is its own 'pair':

  $2 \times 2, 3 \times 3, 4 \times 4$

• • • TIP • • •

- Use differences to find out how the series is formed:

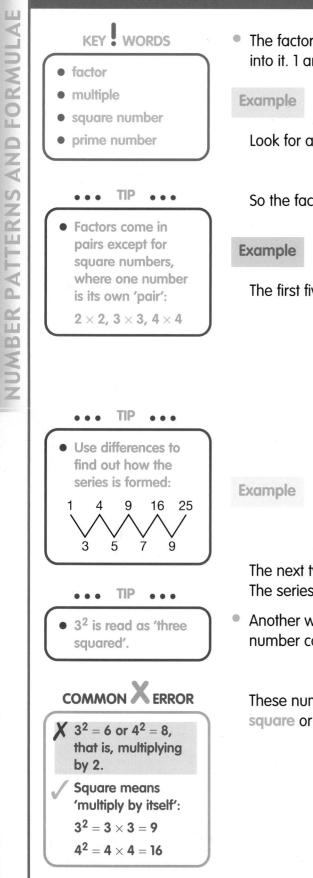

• • • TIP • • •

- 3^2 is read as 'three squared'.

COMMON ✗ ERROR

✗ $3^2 = 6$ or $4^2 = 8$, that is, multiplying by 2.

✓ Square means 'multiply by itself':

$3^2 = 3 \times 3 = 9$

$4^2 = 4 \times 4 = 16$

- The factors of a number are the numbers that divide exactly into it. 1 and the number itself are always factors.

Example Find the factors of 24.

Look for all the products of whole numbers that make 24:

$$1 \times 24, 2 \times 12, 3 \times 8, 4 \times 6.$$

So the factors of 24 are: {1, 2, 3, 4, 6, 8, 12, 24}

Example Write down the first five multiples of 15.

The first five numbers in the 15 times table are:

$$15, 30, 45, 60, 75$$

> The multiples of a number are in its times table.

Example Find the next two numbers in this series and describe how the series is built up:

$$1, 4, 9, 16, 25, \ldots, \ldots$$

The next two terms are 36 and 49.
The series is built up by adding on 3, 5, 7, 9, 11, and so on.

- Another way of spotting this series is to realise that each number can be written as:

$$1 \times 1, 2 \times 2, 3 \times 3, 4 \times 4, 5 \times 5$$

These numbers can be written using a special symbol called square or the power 2 as:

$$1^2, 2^2, 3^2, 4^2, 5^2$$

- The series 1, 4, 9, 16, 25, … is a special series called the **square numbers** because the numbers can be made into square patterns:

- In the mental test, you may be asked questions like:

x squared is 36. What are the possible values of 2 + x?

••• TIP •••

- If $x^2 = 36$, then x could be +6 or −6 but $\sqrt{36} = +6$.

First, x must be +6 or −6, so 2 + 6 = 8 and 2 + −6 = −4
So there are two answers: 8 and −4.

- Typical National Test questions are:

---

1   a   Circle the numbers below that are factors of 60.

    5   10   15   20   25   30

    35   40   45   50   55   60

   b   Solve the equation
$$x^2 - 4 = 60$$

COMMON ✗ ERROR

✗ To only give the answer for the positive square root.

✓ The answer sheet for the mental test will have space for two answers.

ANSWERS

1   a   The numbers that divide into 60 are 5, 10, 15, 20, 30 and 60.

   b x^2 must equal 64, so $x = 8$ or −8.

COMMON ✗ ERROR

✗ Misinterpreting the power, so $x^2 = 2x$

✓ It should mean $x^2 = x \times x$

---

2   From the list below write down:

   a   a square number   b   a multiple of 7

    13   15   17   19   21   23

    25   27   29   31   33   35

ANSWERS

2   a   The only square number in the list is 25.

   b   There are two multiples of 7 in the list: 21 and 35.

Now try Number Patterns and Formulae Quick Check Test 2.

KEY ! WORDS

- term
- expression
- equation
- identity
- variable
- coefficient

••• TIP •••

- $3a = 3 \times a$

  The '$\times$' sign is assumed between a number and a letter.

  Also $\frac{a}{3} = a \div 3$

••• TIP •••

- Replace the letters by the numbers before doing the calculation.

  Don't try to do it in your head:

  If $a = 2$, $b = 6$,

  $a + b = 2 + 6 = 8$

  $3a = 3 \times 2 = 6$

  $b^2 = 6^2 = 36$

COMMON ✗ ERROR

✗ $8a + 2b = 10ab$

✓ You cannot add together terms that contain different letters.

You cannot simplify $8a + 2b$

- Algebra uses letters to represent values in equations, expressions and identities.

- You need to be able to simplify and manipulate algebraic expressions:

  Examples
  $2a + 3a = 5a$
  $3 \times 4a = 12a$
  $4a \times 5b = 20ab$
  $2a \times 3a = 6a^2$
  $3a + 5b + 4a - 3b = 7a + 2b$
  $6a + 4 + 2a + 3 = 8a + 7$

- You also need to be able to substitute numbers into expressions to find a value:

  Example
  If $a = 3$, $b = 4$ and $c = 7$,
  $a + b = 7$
  $2a = 6$
  $4c - 5 = 23$
  $a^2 + b^2 = 25$
  $a(b + c) = 33$

- You also need to be able to interpret expressions:

  Example Imran is x years old. His sister Aisha is 3 years older. His brother Mushtaq is twice as old as Imran.

  a How old is Aisha?
  b How old is Mushtaq?
  c What is the total of their three ages?

  a Aisha is $x + 3$ years old.
  b Mushtaq is $2x$ years old.
  c The total is $x + x + 3 + 2x = 4x + 3$ years

- In the mental test, you may be asked questions like:

Look at the expression $2a + 5b + 6a - 3b$ and simplify it.

Combine the terms containing a, and then the terms containing b.
The answer is $8a + 2b$.

- Some National Test questions are straightforward:

1 Simplify

a $6m + 7 + 2m$

b $6n + 3m + 7n - m$

ANSWERS

1 a Combine like terms:
$6m + 7 + 2m = 8m + 7$

b $6n + 3m + 7n - m = 13n + 2m$

••• TIP •••

- A single letter on its own has a coefficient of 1, but there is no need to write it:

$1m = m$

- Other National Test questions may have a Using and Applying maths element:

2 There are n pupils in Form 7A.

a These expressions show how many pupils are in Forms 7A and 7B. Write the number of pupils in 7C in words.

| 7A | n | pupils |
| 7B | $n + 2$ | pupils |

2 more pupils than 7A
....

| 7A | n | pupils |
| 7C | $n - 3$ | pupils |

....

b Two pupils move from Form 7A to Form 7B.

Write down the number of pupils in Forms 7A and 7B now.

7A has .... pupils. 7B has .... pupils.

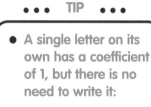
UAM

- This is a Using and Applying maths question. You have to interpret information and use it to find further answers.

ANSWERS

2 a 7C has 3 less pupils than 7A.

b Taking 2 from n gives $n - 2$
and adding 2 to $n + 2$
gives $n + 4$.

7A has $n - 2$ pupils.
7B has $n + 4$ pupils.

$n - 3$ means 'three less than n'.

Now try Number Patterns and Formulae Quick Check Test 3.

KEY **!** WORDS

- formula
- input
- output

••• TIP •••

- A flow diagram can be used to help solve equations:

  $2x + 3 = 21$

  $x = 9$

  $9 \rightarrow \boxed{\times 2} \rightarrow \boxed{+ 3} \rightarrow 21$

- A formula is a rule that changes one number into another.

  For example:

  > ## CAR PARK
  > **£1 plus 50p per hour**

  To park for 4 hours would cost £1 + 4 × £0.50 = £3
  To park for 7 hours would cost £1 + 7 × £0.50 = £4.50
  If it cost £2 to park, the car was there for 2 hours.
  In this case the rule changes the number of hours parking (the input) into the cost of parking (the output).

- Sometimes the formula is more obvious:

INPUT	→	Multiply by 2	→	Add 3	→	OUTPUT

  An input of 6 will give an output of 15.
  An output of 21 had an input of 9.

  > You need to be able to use a formula to find the output given the input, and the input given the output.

••• TIP •••

- Try to write the rule in symbols:

  $T = W \times 30 + 30$

  So, if $W = 6$,

  $T = 6 \times 30 + 30 = 210$

COMMON **✗** ERROR

✗ 210 min
= 2 hours 10 min

✓ 210 min
= 3 hours 30 min, as there are 60 min in an hour.

Example To cook a turkey, use this formula:

> **Cooking time (in min) = Weight of turkey (in kg) × 30 + 30**

a How long will it take to cook a 6 kilogram turkey?

b If a turkey took 5 hours to cook, how much did it weigh?

a Cooking time = 6 × 30 min plus 30 min
   = 210 min = 3 hours 30 min

b 5 hours = 300 minutes
   Deduct 30 minutes: 300 − 30 = 270 minutes
   Divide by 30: 270 ÷ 30 = 9

   The turkey weighed 9 kilograms.

● Typical National Test questions are:

1 The following rule is used to calculate taxi fares.

> £1.20 × distance (in km) plus £2.00

If a fare was £6.80, how long was the journey?

ANSWER

1 Take away the £2.00: £6.80 − £2.00 = £4.80

Divide by £1.20:   £4.80 ÷ £1.20 = 4

The journey was 4 kilometres.

2 The following rule can be used to predict the height of a boy when he is an adult.

> Add 20 cm to the father's height (in cm).
> Add the mother's height (in cm).
> Divide by 2.
> The boy's height will be within 10 cm
> of this measurement.

What will be the range of the adult height of a boy whose father is 174 cm tall and whose mother is 158 cm tall?

ANSWER

2 Add 20 cm to the father's height: 174 + 20 = 194

Add the mother's height: 194 + 158 = 352

Divide by 2:   352 ÷ 2 = 176 cm

The boy's height will be between 166 cm and 186 cm.

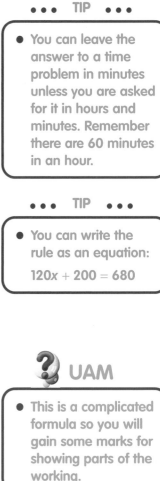

● ● ● **TIP** ● ● ●

● You can leave the answer to a time problem in minutes unless you are asked for it in hours and minutes. Remember there are 60 minutes in an hour.

● ● ● **TIP** ● ● ●

● You can write the rule as an equation:
$120x + 200 = 680$

? **UAM**

● This is a complicated formula so you will gain some marks for showing parts of the working.

Now try Number Patterns and Formulae Quick Check Test 4.

FORMULAE WITH TWO OPERATIONS

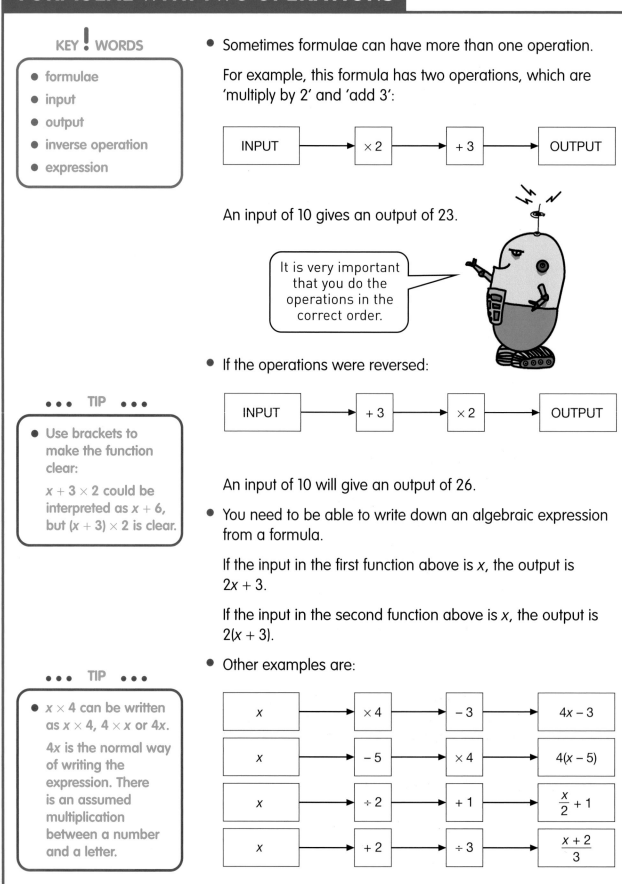

KEY ! WORDS

- formulae
- input
- output
- inverse operation
- expression

- Sometimes formulae can have more than one operation.

  For example, this formula has two operations, which are 'multiply by 2' and 'add 3':

  | INPUT | → | × 2 | → | + 3 | → | OUTPUT |

  An input of 10 gives an output of 23.

  > It is very important that you do the operations in the correct order.

- If the operations were reversed:

  | INPUT | → | + 3 | → | × 2 | → | OUTPUT |

  An input of 10 will give an output of 26.

- You need to be able to write down an algebraic expression from a formula.

  If the input in the first function above is x, the output is $2x + 3$.

  If the input in the second function above is x, the output is $2(x + 3)$.

- Other examples are:

x	→	× 4	→	− 3	→	$4x - 3$
x	→	− 5	→	× 4	→	$4(x - 5)$
x	→	÷ 2	→	+ 1	→	$\frac{x}{2} + 1$
x	→	+ 2	→	÷ 3	→	$\frac{x + 2}{3}$

... TIP ...

- Use brackets to make the function clear:

  $x + 3 \times 2$ could be interpreted as $x + 6$, but $(x + 3) \times 2$ is clear.

... TIP ...

- $x \times 4$ can be written as $x \times 4$, $4 \times x$ or $4x$.

  $4x$ is the normal way of writing the expression. There is an assumed multiplication between a number and a letter.

• Typical National Test questions are:

1 Fill in the missing numbers in the circles below.

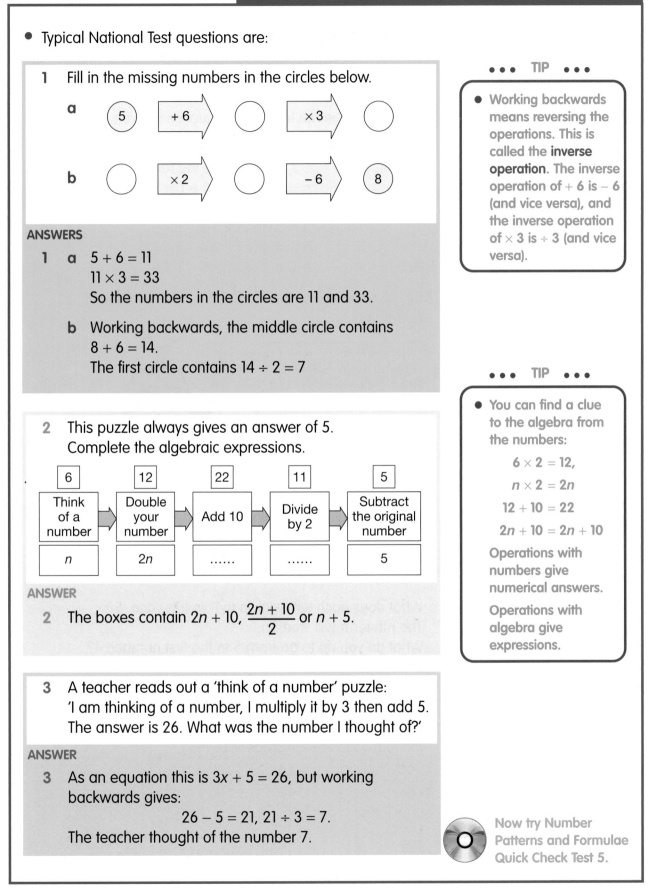

a 5 +6 ○ ×3 ○

b ○ ×2 ○ −6 8

... TIP ...

• Working backwards means reversing the operations. This is called the **inverse operation**. The inverse operation of + 6 is − 6 (and vice versa), and the inverse operation of × 3 is ÷ 3 (and vice versa).

ANSWERS

1 a $5 + 6 = 11$
$11 \times 3 = 33$
So the numbers in the circles are 11 and 33.

b Working backwards, the middle circle contains
$8 + 6 = 14$.
The first circle contains $14 \div 2 = 7$

2 This puzzle always gives an answer of 5.
Complete the algebraic expressions.

6	12	22	11	5
Think of a number	Double your number	Add 10	Divide by 2	Subtract the original number
n	$2n$	……	……	5

... TIP ...

• You can find a clue to the algebra from the numbers:
$6 \times 2 = 12,$
$n \times 2 = 2n$
$12 + 10 = 22$
$2n + 10 = 2n + 10$

Operations with numbers give numerical answers.

Operations with algebra give expressions.

ANSWER

2 The boxes contain $2n + 10$, $\dfrac{2n + 10}{2}$ or $n + 5$.

3 A teacher reads out a 'think of a number' puzzle:
'I am thinking of a number, I multiply it by 3 then add 5. The answer is 26. What was the number I thought of?'

ANSWER

3 As an equation this is $3x + 5 = 26$, but working backwards gives:
$$26 - 5 = 21, \quad 21 \div 3 = 7.$$
The teacher thought of the number 7.

Now try Number Patterns and Formulae Quick Check Test 5.

KEY ! WORDS

- *n*th term

COMMON ✗ ERROR

✗ If the fifth term of the sequence: 2, 5, 8, 11, 14 is 14, then the 10th term is 28.

✓ You cannot just multiply a term. You have to use the rule. The 10th term will be 29.

• • • TIP • • •

- The *n*th term you will be asked to find will always be of the form *an* + *b*:

  $2n + 1$, $4n - 3$

  You will always be given a numerical clue.

- You have already seen how to describe sequences using term-to-term rules. Sequences can also be described using algebraic rules.

Example The *n*th term of a sequence is given by $2n - 1$. Write down the first five terms of the sequence.

Substitute $n = 1, 2, 3, 4$ and 5 into the rule.

$n = 1$ gives $2 \times 1 - 1 = 1$
$n = 2$ gives $2 \times 2 - 1 = 3$
$n = 3$ gives $2 \times 3 - 1 = 5$
$n = 4$ gives $2 \times 4 - 1 = 7$
$n = 5$ gives $2 \times 5 - 1 = 9$.

So the sequence is: 1, 3, 5, 7, 9, ... , which are the odd numbers.

The *n*th term is useful for finding out a number in a sequence without writing out all the sequence.

- There is a quick way of finding out the *n*th term:

Example Find the *n*th term of the sequence 4, 9, 14, 19, 24, 29, ...

What does each term go up by? In this case, 5.
The *n*th term will start 5*n*.
What do you do to go from 5 to the first number, 4? In this case, minus 1.
The *n*th term will be 5*n* minus 1 or $5n - 1$.

- So for the sequence 4, 7, 10, 13, 16, ... the terms increase in steps of 3.

  $3 + 1 = 4$, so the *n*th term is $3n + 1$.

- In the mental test, you may be asked questions like:

The *n*th term of a sequence is $\frac{1}{2}(n + 2)^2$. What is the 4th term of the sequence?

Substitute 4 for *n*:

$$\frac{1}{2}(4 + 2)^2 = \frac{1}{2} \times 6^2 = \frac{1}{2} \times 36 = 18$$

- National Test questions often involve a diagram:

1 The following patterns are made up of black and white hexagons.

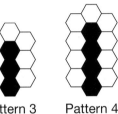

Pattern 1   Pattern 2   Pattern 3   Pattern 4

Complete this table.

Pattern	Black hexagons	White hexagons
5		
10		
n		

••• TIP •••

- Write out the sequence of numbers as a list. This will help you to see the *n*th term:

Black hexagons:
1   2   3   4   5

So the *n*th term is *n*.

White hexagons:
3   5   7   9   11

So the *n*th term is $2n + 1$.

ANSWERS

1 The fifth pattern has 5 black hexagons and 11 white hexagons.

You should realise that the number of black hexagons is the same as the pattern number and the number of white hexagons is double the pattern number plus 1.

So the table is:

Pattern	Black hexagons	White hexagons
5	5	11
10	10	21
n	*n*	$2n + 1$

Now try Number Patterns and Formulae Quick Check Test 6.

Also try Number Patterns and Formulae Final Test.

COORDINATES IN THE FIRST QUADRANT

- *x*-coordinate
- *y*-coordinate
- origin
- *x*-axis
- *y*-axis

COMMON ✗ ERROR

✗ Reading and plotting coordinates the wrong way round.

✓ The *x*-coordinate is always given first, followed by the *y*-coordinate.

- Coordinates are used to describe the position of a point on a grid.

For example, the point A has coordinates (4, 3) and B has coordinates (1, 4).

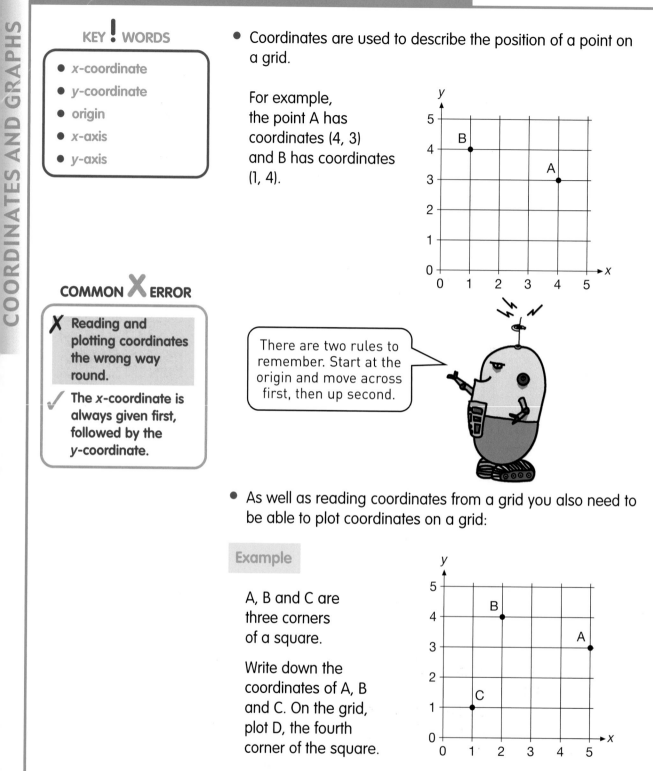

There are two rules to remember. Start at the origin and move across first, then up second.

- As well as reading coordinates from a grid you also need to be able to plot coordinates on a grid:

Example

A, B and C are three corners of a square.

Write down the coordinates of A, B and C. On the grid, plot D, the fourth corner of the square.

A is (5, 3), B is (2, 4) and C is (1, 1).

D should be plotted at the point (4, 0).

● In the mental test, you may be asked questions like:

Look at the grid. What are the coordinates of the midpoint of AB?

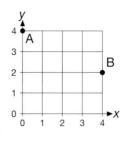

You can see from the grid that the midpoint is (2, 3).

● Typical National Test questions are:

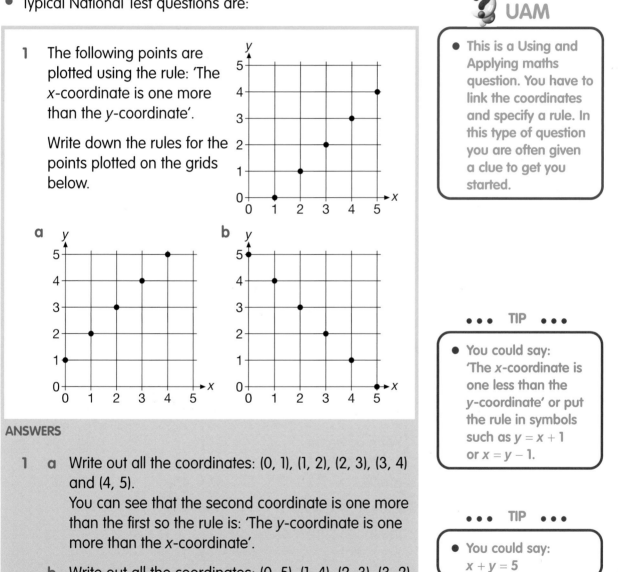

1 The following points are plotted using the rule: 'The *x*-coordinate is one more than the *y*-coordinate'.

Write down the rules for the points plotted on the grids below.

a

b

? UAM

● This is a Using and Applying maths question. You have to link the coordinates and specify a rule. In this type of question you are often given a clue to get you started.

● ● ● **TIP** ● ● ●

● You could say: 'The *x*-coordinate is one less than the *y*-coordinate' or put the rule in symbols such as $y = x + 1$ or $x = y - 1$.

ANSWERS

1 a Write out all the coordinates: (0, 1), (1, 2), (2, 3), (3, 4) and (4, 5).
You can see that the second coordinate is one more than the first so the rule is: 'The *y*-coordinate is one more than the *x*-coordinate'.

b Write out all the coordinates: (0, 5), (1, 4), (2, 3), (3, 2), (4, 1), (5, 0).
You can see that the coordinates add up to 5 so 'the sum of the *x*- and *y*-coordinates is 5'.

● ● ● **TIP** ● ● ●

● You could say: $x + y = 5$

Now try Coordinates and Graphs Quick Check Test 1.

COORDINATES IN ALL FOUR QUADRANTS

KEY ! WORDS

- quadrant
- *x*-coordinate
- *y*-coordinate
- origin
- *x*-axis
- *y*-axis

... TIP ...

- Read the value from the *x*-axis first, and the value from the *y*-axis second.

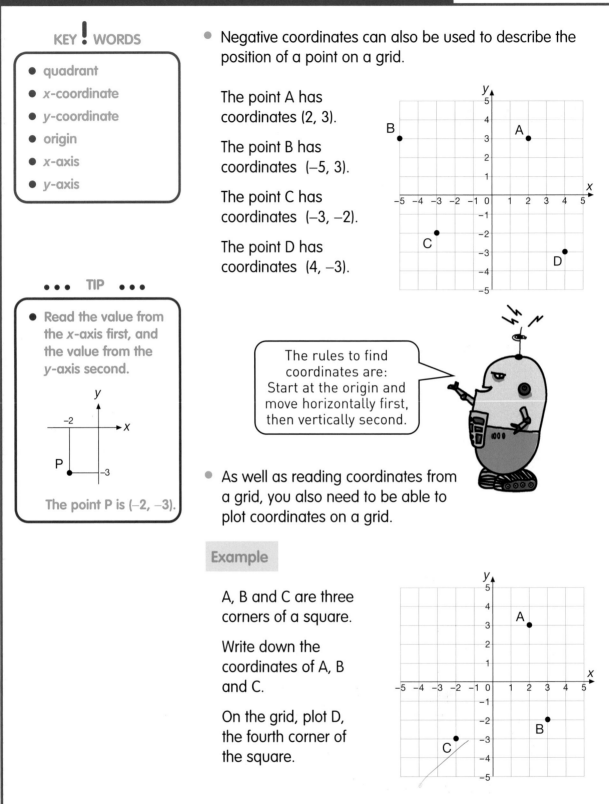

The point P is (−2, −3).

- Negative coordinates can also be used to describe the position of a point on a grid.

The point A has coordinates (2, 3).

The point B has coordinates (−5, 3).

The point C has coordinates (−3, −2).

The point D has coordinates (4, −3).

The rules to find coordinates are: Start at the origin and move horizontally first, then vertically second.

- As well as reading coordinates from a grid, you also need to be able to plot coordinates on a grid.

Example

A, B and C are three corners of a square.

Write down the coordinates of A, B and C.

On the grid, plot D, the fourth corner of the square.

A is (2, 3), B is (3, −2) and C is (−2, −3).

D should be plotted at the point (−3, 2).

● In the mental test, you may be asked questions like:

Look at the grid. What are the coordinates of A?

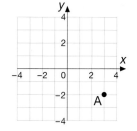

You can see from the grid that the point is (3, −2).

● Typical National Test questions are:

1 Look at the diagram.

a The point M is halfway between points B and C. What are the coordinates of M?

b The shape ABCD is a kite. What are the coordinates of point D?

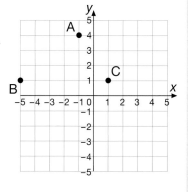

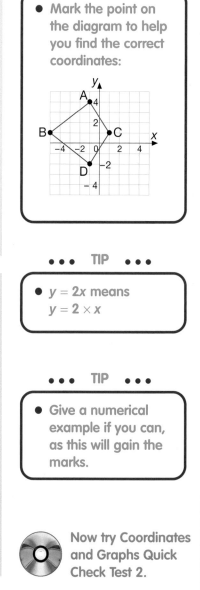

ANSWERS

1 a B is (−5, 1), C is (1, 1), so M is (−2, 1).

b D is the point (−1, −2).

2 The graph shows the line $y = 2x$.

a Write down the coordinates of the points A and B.

b The point C (−8, −16) also lies on the line. Explain how you know this is true.

ANSWERS

1 a A is (1, 2) and B is (−2, −4)

b The y-value is twice the x-value.
$$2 \times -8 = -16$$

... **TIP** ...

● Mark the point on the diagram to help you find the correct coordinates:

... **TIP** ...

● $y = 2x$ means
$y = 2 \times x$

... **TIP** ...

● Give a numerical example if you can, as this will gain the marks.

Now try Coordinates and Graphs Quick Check Test 2.

USING COORDINATES FOR GRAPHS

... TIP ...

- Always label graphs.

- Graphs show the relationship between variables on a coordinate grid.

  For example, the equation $y = 2x + 1$ shows a relationship between x and y such that the y-value is 2 times the x-value plus 1.

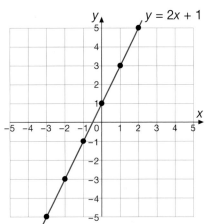

If $x = 0$, $y = 2 \times 0 + 1 = 1$. This can be represented by the coordinates (0, 1).

- Similarly, when $x = 1$, $y = 2 \times 1 + 1 = 3$. This is the point (1, 3).

  Other coordinates connecting x and y are (−3, −5), (−1, −1), (2, 5), etc.

  When these are plotted on a graph, they can be joined by a straight line.

- Coordinates are always given in the order: (x, y).

... TIP ...

- You can also plot graphs using the gradient intercept method:

  In an equation like $y = mx + c$, c is where the graph crosses the y-axis and m is the gradient.

  So, for $y = 3x - 1$, the graph crosses the y-axis at −1 and has a gradient of 3. This means for every 1 unit across, the graph goes up by 3 units.

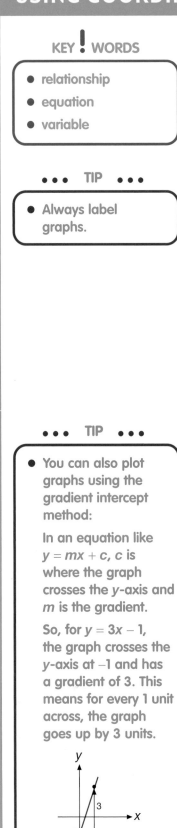

Example Draw the graph of $y = 3x - 1$.

First find some points by choosing x-values:

Let $x = 0$, $y = 3 \times 0 - 1 = -1$

Let $x = 1$, $y = 3 \times 1 - 1 = 2$

Let $x = 2$, $y = 3 \times 2 - 1 = 5$

Let $x = -1$, $y = 3 \times -1 - 1 = -4$

Plot the points and join them up.

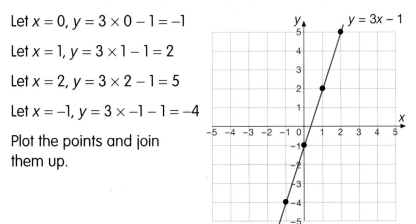

- In the mental test, you may be asked questions like:

Look at the equation
$y = 3x + 2$.
What is the value of
y when $x = 2$?

Substitute $x = 2$ into the equation, so $y = 3 \times 2 + 2 = 8$

- Typical National Test questions are:

1 The graph shows a straight line.
The equation of the line is $y = 2x$.
Does the point (35, 65) lie on the line?

Explain how you know.

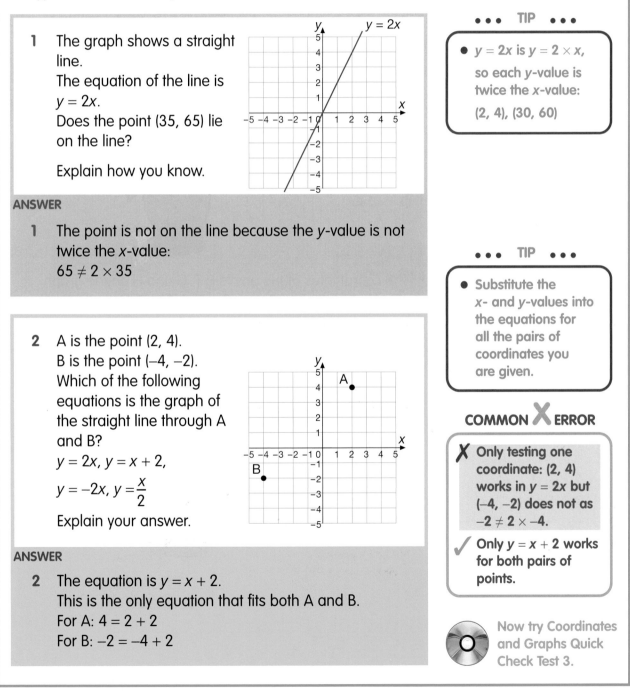

... TIP ...

- $y = 2x$ is $y = 2 \times x$, so each y-value is twice the x-value:
(2, 4), (30, 60)

ANSWER

1 The point is not on the line because the y-value is not twice the x-value:
$65 \neq 2 \times 35$

... TIP ...

- Substitute the x- and y-values into the equations for all the pairs of coordinates you are given.

2 A is the point (2, 4).
B is the point (−4, −2).
Which of the following equations is the graph of the straight line through A and B?
$y = 2x$, $y = x + 2$,
$y = -2x$, $y = \dfrac{x}{2}$

Explain your answer.

COMMON ✗ ERROR

✗ Only testing one coordinate: (2, 4) works in $y = 2x$ but (−4, −2) does not as $-2 \neq 2 \times -4$.

✓ Only $y = x + 2$ works for both pairs of points.

ANSWER

2 The equation is $y = x + 2$.
This is the only equation that fits both A and B.
For A: $4 = 2 + 2$
For B: $-2 = -4 + 2$

Now try Coordinates and Graphs Quick Check Test 3.

COORDINATES AND GRAPHS

lines of the form:

- $x = a$
- $y = b$
- $x + y = c$

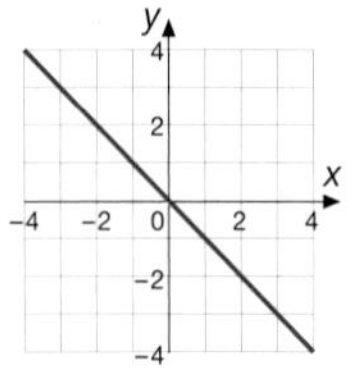

- There are some graphs that you need to learn.

- The coordinates of the points A, B, C and D are $(-5, 3)$, $(-3, 3)$, $(0, 3)$, $(4, 3)$ respectively.

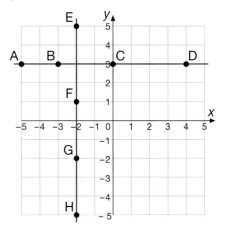

  You can see that they all have a y-coordinate of 3 and form a straight line on the grid.

  This line has an equation $y = 3$.

• • • TIP • • •

- Two other graphs that you need to know are:

$y = x$

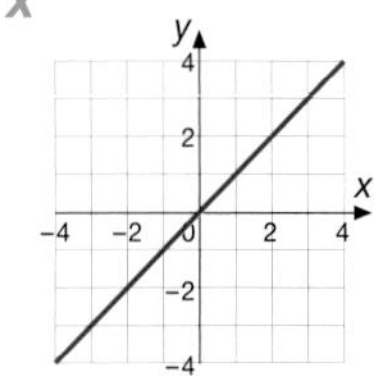

and $y = -x$.

All lines of the form $y = b$ are horizontal.

- The coordinates of the points E, F, G and H on the graph above are $(-2, 5)$, $(-2, 1)$, $(-2, -2)$, $(-2, -5)$ respectively.

  You can see that they all have a x-coordinate of -2 and form a straight line on the grid.

  This line has an equation $x = -2$.

All lines of the form $x = a$ are vertical.

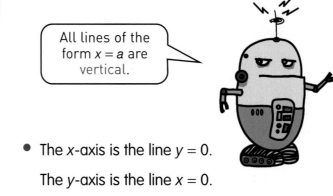

- The x-axis is the line $y = 0$.

  The y-axis is the line $x = 0$.

- The coordinates of the points A, B, C and D are (−3, 5), (0, 2), (3, −1), (5, −3) respectively.

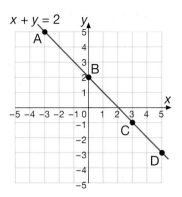

  You can see that the x- and y-coordinates add up to a total of 2.
  This line has an equation $x + y = 2$.

- All lines of the form $x + y = c$ slope at 45° from top left to bottom right, and pass through the value c on both axes.

- Typical National Test questions are:

1 The graph shows a triangle.

   a What is the equation of the line through A and B?

   b What is the equation of the line through A and C?

   c What is the equation of the line through B and C?

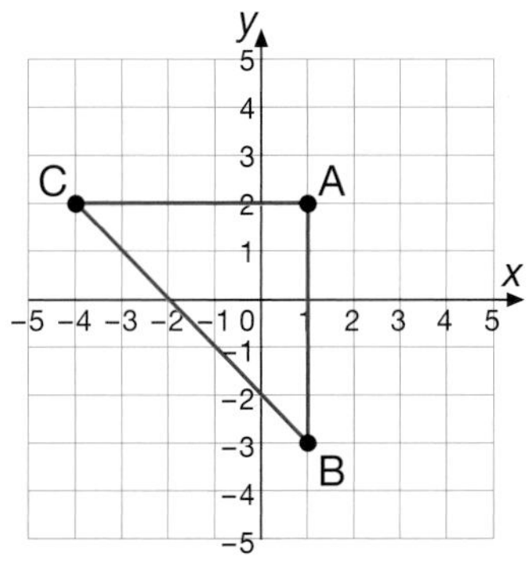

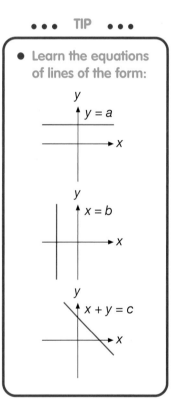

... TIP ...

- Learn the equations of lines of the form:

$y = a$

$x = b$

$x + y = c$

ANSWERS

1 a $x = 1$. AB is a vertical line through 1 on the x-axis.
   b $y = 2$. AC is a horizontal line through 2 on the y-axis.
   c $x + y = -2$. The line passes through (0, −2) and (−2, 0).

2 A is the point (0, 5), which lies on the line $x + y = 5$. Give another point on the line.

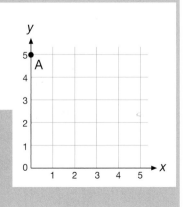

ANSWER

2 There are lots of answers: (1, 4), (2, 3), (3, 2), (4, 1), (0, 5)

Now try Coordinates and Graphs Quick Check Test 4.

Also try Coordinates and Graphs Final Test.

BODMAS AND BRACKETS

KEY ! WORDS

- BODMAS
- order
- powers
- brackets

COMMON ✗ ERROR

✗ Working out 2×3^2 as 3^6, because $2 \times 3 = 6$ which is then squared.

✓ The power should be found first, so $3^2 = 9$.

This value is then multiplied by 2, so $2 \times 3^2 = 18$.

COMMON ✗ ERROR

✗ Doing operations in order rather than by the rules of BODMAS:
$3 + 2 \times 6 = 30$, because $3 + 2 = 5$ and $5 \times 6 = 30$.

✓ It should be:
$2 \times 6 \ (= 12)$ first, and then $3 + 12 = 15$.

- To calculate $2 + 3 \times 4$, work out 3×4 first and then add this to 2 to give 14. This calculation uses the rules of mathematical operations, which is known as BODMAS.

- **BODMAS** stands for **B**rackets, **O**rder, **D**ivision, **M**ultiplication, **A**ddition, **S**ubtraction.

  This is the order in which operations must be done.

  For example:
  Brackets are always worked out first.
  Powers are always worked out before multiplication.

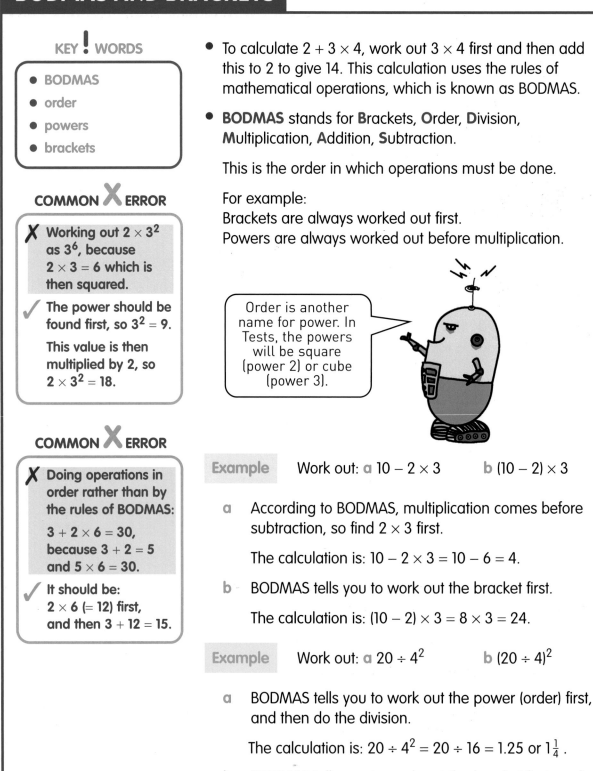

Order is another name for power. In Tests, the powers will be square (power 2) or cube (power 3).

Example   Work out: a $10 - 2 \times 3$ b $(10 - 2) \times 3$

a   According to BODMAS, multiplication comes before subtraction, so find 2×3 first.

The calculation is: $10 - 2 \times 3 = 10 - 6 = 4$.

b   BODMAS tells you to work out the bracket first.

The calculation is: $(10 - 2) \times 3 = 8 \times 3 = 24$.

Example   Work out: a $20 \div 4^2$ b $(20 \div 4)^2$

a   BODMAS tells you to work out the power (order) first, and then do the division.

The calculation is: $20 \div 4^2 = 20 \div 16 = 1.25$ or $1\frac{1}{4}$.

b   BODMAS tells you to work out the bracket first, and then find the power.

The calculation is: $(20 \div 4)^2 = 5^2 = 25$.

- In the mental test, you may be asked questions like:

Look at the expression $3m^2$. What is the value of the expression when $m = 10$?

Using BODMAS, $3m^2 = 3 \times m^2 = 3 \times 10^2 = 3 \times 100 = 300$

- Typical National Test questions are:

1   a   Write the answers to:
     i $(5 + 3) \times 4$ ii $5 + (3 \times 4)$

   b   Work out the answer to: $(8 - 3) \times (4^2 \div 2)$

   c   i   Put brackets in the calculation to make the answer correct:
      $16 \div 2 + 6 \times 4 = 8$

     ii   Put brackets in the calculation to make the answer correct:
      $16 \div 2 + 6 \times 4 = 56$

ANSWERS

1   a   Using the rules of BODMAS the answers are:

     i $8 \times 4 = 32$ ii $5 + 12 = 17$

   b   Work out the brackets first. Within the second bracket, the power should be calculated first.

     $(8 - 3) \times (4^2 \div 2) = 5 \times (16 \div 2) = 5 \times 8 = 40$

   c   Trying brackets in various places gives:

     i $16 \div (2 + 6) \times 4 = 16 \div 8 \times 4 = 2 \times 4 = 8$

     ii $(16 \div 2 + 6) \times 4 = (8 + 6) \times 4 = 14 \times 4 = 56$

•••   **TIP**   •••

- Try brackets in various places until you find the correct answer:

$(16 \div 2) + 6 \times 4 = 32$

$16 \div (2 + 6) \times 4 = 8$

Now try Solving Equations Quick Check Test 1.

SOLVING EQUATIONS

KEY ! WORDS

- equation
- solve
- variable
- inverse operation

... TIP ...

- There are different ways of writing the solution to an equation, but they all arrive at the same solution:

$$2x + 6 - 6 = 12 - 6$$
$$2x = 6$$
$$2x \div 2 = 6 \div 2$$
$$x = 3$$

This shows the working in detail.

... TIP ...

- You will hear rules such as: 'Change sides, change signs' and 'What you do to one side, you do to the other'. These all mean 'perform the inverse operation'.

• 'I am thinking of a number. I double it and add 6. The answer is 12. What was the number I thought of?'

This type of question can usually be solved in your head to give the answer 3.

It can also be written as an **equation**.

An equation is an expression involving a certain letter, x say, that is equal to a number. 'Solving the equation' means finding the value of x that makes it true.

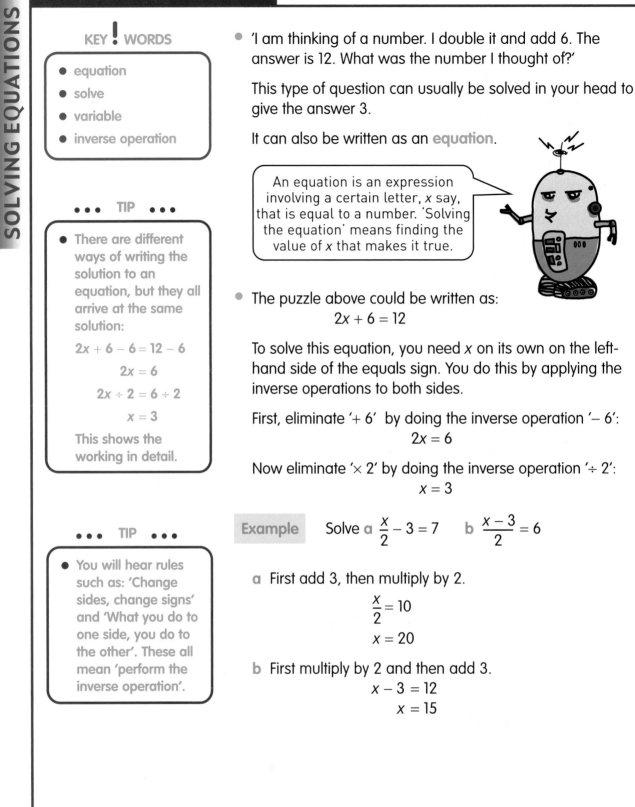

• The puzzle above could be written as:
$$2x + 6 = 12$$

To solve this equation, you need x on its own on the left-hand side of the equals sign. You do this by applying the inverse operations to both sides.

First, eliminate '+ 6' by doing the inverse operation '− 6':
$$2x = 6$$

Now eliminate '× 2' by doing the inverse operation '÷ 2':
$$x = 3$$

Example Solve a $\dfrac{x}{2} - 3 = 7$ b $\dfrac{x - 3}{2} = 6$

a First add 3, then multiply by 2.
$$\frac{x}{2} = 10$$
$$x = 20$$

b First multiply by 2 and then add 3.
$$x - 3 = 12$$
$$x = 15$$

- In the mental test, you may be asked questions like:

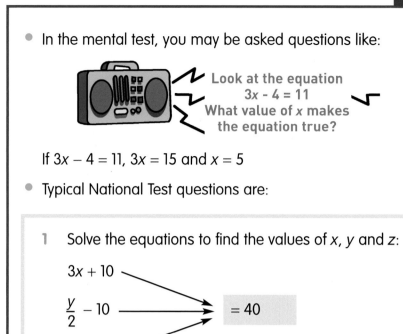

Look at the equation
$3x - 4 = 11$
What value of x makes the equation true?

If $3x - 4 = 11$, $3x = 15$ and $x = 5$

- Typical National Test questions are:

1 Solve the equations to find the values of x, y and z:

$3x + 10$

$\dfrac{y}{2} - 10$ ———→ $= 40$

$z^2 + 4$

ANSWERS

1 $3x + 10 = 40 \Rightarrow 3x = 30 \Rightarrow x = 10$

$\dfrac{y}{2} - 10 = 40 \Rightarrow \dfrac{y}{2} = 50 \Rightarrow y = 100$

$z^2 + 4 = 40 \Rightarrow z^2 = 36 \Rightarrow z = 6$ (or -6)

2 This formula shows how a taxi firm works out its fares:

| $F = £0.80k + £1.20$ | $F =$ Fare in pounds |
| | $k =$ distance in kilometres |

If a fare is £3.60, how far was the journey?

ANSWER

2 Set up the equation (in pence)

$$80k + 120 = 360$$

$$80k = 240$$

$$k = 3 \text{ kilometres}$$

COMMON ✗ ERROR

✗ Eliminating operations in the wrong order:

$$\dfrac{x + 2}{3} = 4$$

$$\dfrac{x}{3} = 2$$

$$x = 6$$

Here the inverse operations − 2 and × 3 have been applied in the wrong order.

✓ The correct order is × 3 then − 2:

$$x + 2 = 12$$

$$x = 10$$

• • • TIP • • •

- Always check that your answer works in the original equation:

$3 \times 10 + 10 = 40$ ✓

$100 \div 2 - 10 = 40$ ✓

$6^2 + 4 = 40$ ✓

• • • TIP • • •

- Sometimes it is easier to work in pence than pounds.

Now try Solving Equations Quick Check Test 2.

KEY **!** WORDS

- equation
- solve
- variable
- inverse operation

••• TIP •••

- Rearrange the equation before working anything out. If you try to rearrange and work out at the same time, you may make a mistake.

••• TIP •••

- This is an example of 'Change sides, change signs'.

  The working in full is:

  $3x + 6 = x + 10$

  $3x - x + 6 - 6 =$
  $\quad x - x + 10 - 6$

COMMON ✗ ERROR

✗ Rearranging and not changing signs:

$5x + 6 = 3x + 18$
$5x + 3x = 18 + 6$
$\quad\quad 8x = 24$
$\quad\quad\quad x = 3$

Check

LHS $= 5 \times 3 + 6 = 21$
RHS $= 3 \times 3 + 18 = 27$

✓ It should be:

$5x - 3x = 18 - 6$
$\quad\quad 2x = 12$
$\quad\quad\; x = 6$

Check

LHS $= 5 \times 6 + 6 = 36$
RHS $= 3 \times 6 + 18 = 36$

- 'I am thinking of a number. I treble it and add 6. The answer is 10 more than the original number. What was the number I thought of?'

  The answer is 2, but this type of question is difficult to solve in your head.

- The puzzle above could also be written as an equation:

  $$3x + 6 = x + 10$$

To solve this you need to have x on its own on the left-hand side of the equals sign. To do this, first move all the x terms to the left-hand side and all the number terms to the right-hand side.

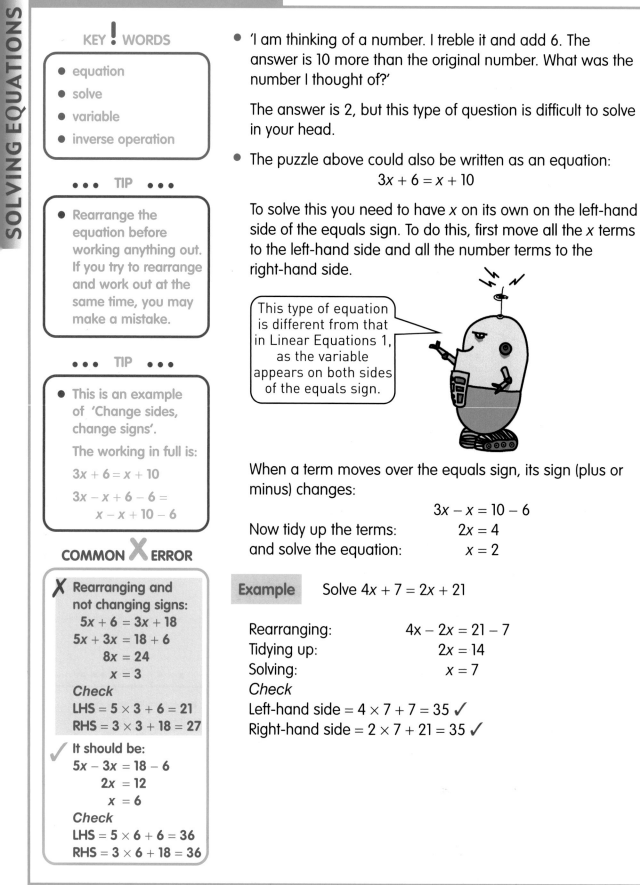

This type of equation is different from that in Linear Equations 1, as the variable appears on both sides of the equals sign.

When a term moves over the equals sign, its sign (plus or minus) changes:

$$3x - x = 10 - 6$$

Now tidy up the terms: $\quad 2x = 4$
and solve the equation: $\quad\; x = 2$

Example Solve $4x + 7 = 2x + 21$

Rearranging: $\quad\quad\quad 4x - 2x = 21 - 7$
Tidying up: $\quad\quad\quad\quad\quad 2x = 14$
Solving: $\quad\quad\quad\quad\quad\quad\; x = 7$
Check
Left-hand side $= 4 \times 7 + 7 = 35$ ✓
Right-hand side $= 2 \times 7 + 21 = 35$ ✓

- National Test questions are usually straightforward, such as:

---

1 Solve the equations:

a $4s + 7 = s + 25$

b $12x + 30 = 6x + 33$

ANSWERS

1 a Rearrange: $4s - s = 25 - 7$

$$3s = 18$$

$$s = 6$$

Check $4 \times 6 + 7 = 31$, $6 + 25 = 31$, so LHS = RHS.

b Rearrange: $12x - 6x = 33 - 30$

$$6x = 3$$

$$x = \tfrac{1}{2}$$

Check $12 \times \tfrac{1}{2} + 30 = 36$, $6 \times \tfrac{1}{2} + 33 = 36$, so LHS = RHS.

COMMON **ERROR**

✗ Solving $4x = 2$ as $x = 2$.

✓ The answer should be:
$4x \div 4 = 2 \div 4$,
so $x = \tfrac{1}{2}$ or **0.5**

---

2 This formula shows the accurate conversion from degrees Fahrenheit, $F°$, to degrees Centigrade, $C°$:

$$F = 1.8C + 32$$

This formula shows the approximate conversion from degrees Fahrenheit, $F°$ to degrees Centigrade, $C°$:

$$F = 2C + 30$$

For what temperature in degrees Centigrade do the two formulae give the same values?

? UAM

- This is a Using and Applying maths question. You need to equate both formulae and then solve the resulting equation.

ANSWERS

2 Form the equation where both are equal:

$$2C + 30 = 1.8C + 32$$

Rearrange: $2C - 1.8C = 32 - 30$

$$0.2C = 2$$

$$C = 10$$

 Now try Solving Equations Quick Check Test 3.

FRACTIONAL EQUATIONS

KEY ! WORDS

- fractional equation
- solve
- variable
- inverse operation
- cross-multiply

••• TIP •••

- You can remember cross-multiplying by thinking of

$$\frac{x}{2} \diagdown = \diagup \frac{7}{4}$$

which is where the term 'cross' comes from.

- A fractional equation is one in which the variable appears as the numerator or denominator of a fraction.

Example Solve the equation $\dfrac{x}{2} = \dfrac{7}{4}$

The first step in solving a fractional equation is to cross-multiply. This means multiply the denominator of the left-hand side by the numerator of the right-hand side and multiply the denominator of the right-hand side by the numerator of the left-hand side.

So: $4 \times x = 2 \times 7$

Tidy up the terms: $4x = 14$

Solve the equation: $x = 3\frac{1}{2}$ or 3.5

- You may just write down $4x = 14$ and then solve the equation.

- Answers can be left as top-heavy fractions, such as $\frac{14}{4} = \frac{7}{2}$, unless you are asked for an answer in its simplest form.

Example Solve the equation $\dfrac{2}{x} = \dfrac{7}{11}$

Cross-multiplying: $22 = 7x$

This equation has the x-term on the right so reverse the equation: $7x = 22$

Divide by 7: $x = \frac{22}{7} = 3\frac{1}{7}$

Example Solve the equation $\dfrac{8}{9} = \dfrac{4}{x}$

Cross-multiplying: $8x = 36$

Divide by 8: $x = \frac{36}{8} = 4\frac{1}{2}$

- National Test questions are usually straightforward, such as:

---

1 Solve these equations.

a $\dfrac{3}{4} = \dfrac{t}{8}$

b $\dfrac{2}{5} = \dfrac{7}{x}$

ANSWERS

1 a Cross-multiply: $24 = 4t$

Rearrange: $4t = 24$

Solve: $t = 6$

b Cross-multiply: $2x = 35$

Solve: $x = \dfrac{35}{2}$

$x = 17\tfrac{1}{2}$

 UAM

- This is a Using and Applying maths question. You have to realise you need to set up a fractional equation.

---

2 Mary has x counters in a bag.

She removes 5 counters and then shares the rest into 4 equal piles.

Each pile contains 8 counters.

What is the value of x?

ANSWERS

2 Set up the equation: $\dfrac{x-5}{4} = 8$

Cross-multiply: $x - 5 = 32$

Solve: $x = 37$

Now try Solving Equations Quick Check Test 4.

TRIAL AND IMPROVEMENT

- trial and improvement

COMMON ✗ ERROR

✗ Miscalculating a cube e.g. $2.5^3 = 7.5$

✓ It should be
$2.5^3 = 2.5 \times 2.5 \times 2.5$
$= 15.625$

• • • TIP • • •

- This type of question will be on Paper 2. Make sure you can use your calculator to work out cubes.

COMMON ✗ ERROR

✗ Not testing the middle value.

✓ Unless you test this, you cannot be sure which value is closer to the actual answer.

- The only way to solve an equation like

$x^3 + 2x = 27$

is by trial and improvement.

Trial and improvement is just sensible guesswork.

Example

- There is a solution of the equation $x^3 + 2x = 27$ between 2 and 3. Find the solution to 1 decimal place.

- Start by making a guess between 2 and 3:

| 2.5 is a sensible guess. | $2.5^3 + 2 \times 2.5 = 20.625$ |

| Then make a better guess: | $2.6^3 + 2 \times 2.6 = 22.776$ |

Keep on making better guesses: $2.7^3 + 2 \times 2.7 = 25.083$

$2.8^3 + 2 \times 2.8 = 27.552$

When you find two 1 d.p. values that 'bracket' the answer, check the middle value to make sure which of the values is the closer.

$2.75^3 + 2 \times 2.75 = 26.296\ 875$

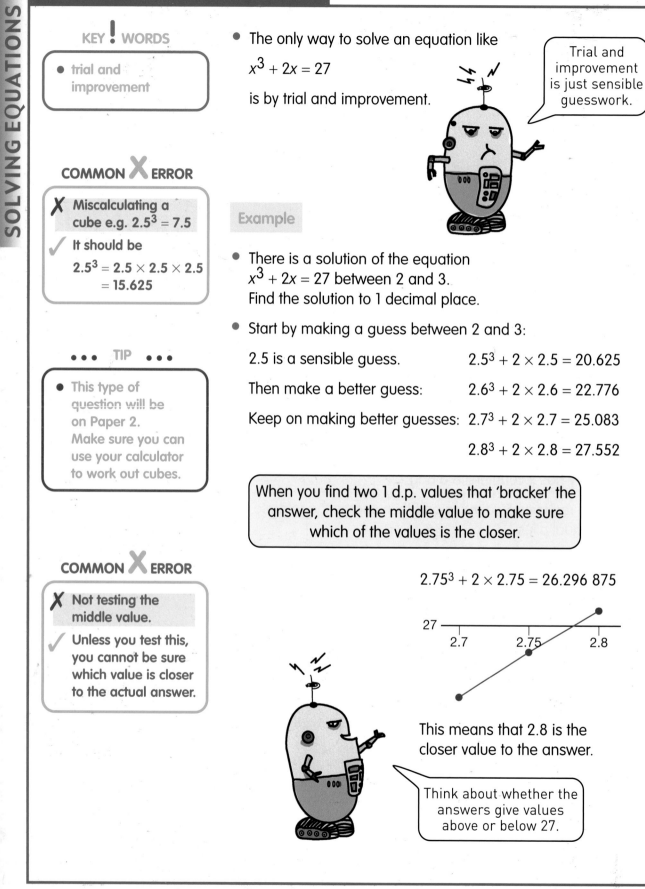

This means that 2.8 is the closer value to the answer.

Think about whether the answers give values above or below 27.

• National Test questions usually give a table to do your working in and give you a starting value.

1   A rectangle has a side of length y centimetres.
     The other side is of length $y + 3$ centimetres.

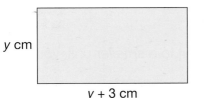

y cm

y + 3 cm

The area of the rectangle is 48.16 cm^2.
This equation shows the area of the rectangle.
$y(y + 3) = 48.16$

Find the value of y.

y	$y + 3$	$y(y + 3)$	Comment
4	7	28	Too low

... TIP ...

• One value is always given. (Sometimes two values will be given.)

Check this value to make sure you can do the calculation on your calculator correctly.

This also gives you a clue as to which value to test next.

ANSWER

1   The given starting value of 4 gives an area that is too low.

Continue the table with a higher value than 4.

y	$y + 3$	$y(y + 3)$	Comment
4	7	28	Too low
5	8	40	Too low
6	9	54	Too high
5.5	8.5	46.75	Too low
5.6	8.6	48.16	Exact

Because the answer is exact there is no need to test a half-way value.

Now try Solving Equations Quick Check 5.

Also try Solving Equations Final Test.

METRIC UNITS

- kilometre (km)
- metre (m)
- centimetre (cm)
- millimetre (mm)
- kilogram (kg)
- gram (g)
- tonne
- litre (l)
- centilitre (cl)
- millilitre (ml)

••• TIP •••

- Learn what the prefixes mean:

  milli- = ÷ 1000

  centi- = ÷ 100

  kilo- = × 1000

••• TIP •••

- When multiplying or dividing by 10, 100 or 1000, remember to move the digits the correct number of places to the left or to the right.

- These are the metric units you need to know:

Units of length	Units of weight	Units of capacity
10 mm = 1 cm	1000 g = 1 kg	10 ml = 1 cl
1000 mm = 1 m	1000 kg = 1 tonne	1000 ml = 1 l
100 cm = 1 m		100 cl = 1 l
1000 m = 1 km		

- To change from a *large* unit to a *smaller* unit, you need to multiply.

- To change from a *small* unit to a *larger* unit you need to divide.

Example   Change 3.2 m into centimetres.

Large unit to a smaller unit, so multiply by 100:
$$3.2 \, m = 3.2 \times 100 = 320 \, cm$$

Example   Change 2500 g into kilograms.

Small unit to a larger unit, so divide by 1000:
$$2500 \, g = 2500 \div 1000 = 2.5 \, kg$$

- In the mental test, you may be asked questions like:

How many millilitres are there in a litre?

You should know that there are 1000 millilitres in a litre.

- National Test questions are straightforward, such as:

1 Fill in the gaps below:

   a   3 m = ... cm = ... mm

   b   0.5 l = ... cl = ... ml

   c   1.25 kg = ... g

ANSWERS

1   a   3 m = 300 cm = 3000 mm

   b   0.5 l = 50 cl = 500 ml

   c   1.25 kg = 1250 g

- Sometimes National Test questions test your ability to read scales:

2 Write down the value from each of the following scales.

   a

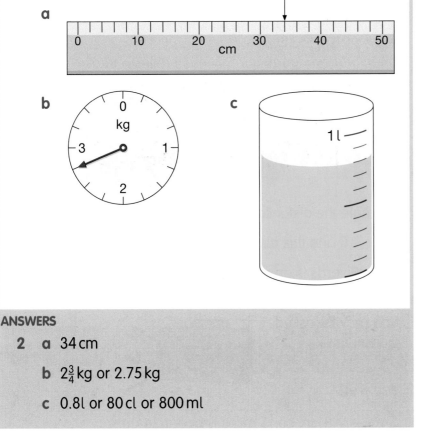

ANSWERS

2   a   34 cm

   b $2\frac{3}{4}$ kg or 2.75 kg

   c   0.8 l or 80 cl or 800 ml

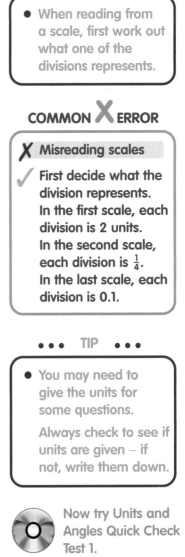

••• TIP •••

- When reading from a scale, first work out what one of the divisions represents.

COMMON ✗ ERROR

✗ Misreading scales

✓ First decide what the division represents. In the first scale, each division is 2 units. In the second scale, each division is $\frac{1}{4}$. In the last scale, each division is 0.1.

••• TIP •••

- You may need to give the units for some questions.

  Always check to see if units are given – if not, write them down.

Now try Units and Angles Quick Check Test 1.

IMPERIAL UNITS

- mile (m)
- yard (yd)
- foot (ft)
- inch (in)
- stone (st)
- pound (lb)
- ounce (oz)
- gallon
- pint

- Some imperial units are still in common use in Britain:

I am 5ft 8in tall and weigh 11¹/₂ stone.

I am 1.52m tall and weigh 45kg.

- These are the imperial units you need to know:

Units of length	Units of weight	Units of capacity
12 in = 1 ft	16 oz = 1 lb	8 pints = 1 gallon
3 ft = 1 yd	14 lb = 1 st	

You need to learn the approximations between imperial units and metric units. The symbol '≈' means 'is approximately equal to'.

$$1\,m \approx 3\,ft$$
$$1\,kg \approx 2\tfrac{1}{4}\,lb$$
$$1\,l \approx 1\tfrac{3}{4}\,pints$$

$$1\,in \approx 2\tfrac{1}{2}\,cm$$
$$5\ miles \approx 8\,km$$
$$1\,oz \approx 30\,g$$
$$1\ gallon \approx 4\tfrac{1}{2}\,l$$

- Always remember to write the correct units at each stage.

Example

Sunbeach Hotel 600 yards

Estimate the distance to the hotel in metres.

1m ≈ 3 ft and this also means 1m ≈ 1yd.

So 600 yards is approximately 600 metres.

- In the mental test, you may be asked questions like:

How many kilometres are about the same as 15 miles?

5 miles ≈ 8 km, so 15 miles is about 24 km.

- National Test questions are straightforward, such as:

  1 a Change 12 inches into centimetres.

     b Change $1\frac{1}{2}$ pounds into grams.

ANSWERS

  1 a $1\,\text{in} \approx 2\frac{1}{2}\,\text{cm}$, so $12\,\text{in} \approx 12 \times 2\frac{1}{2} \approx 30\,\text{cm}$

     b $1\,\text{lb} = 16\,\text{oz}$, so $1\frac{1}{2}\,\text{lb} = 24\,\text{oz}$

        $1\,\text{oz} \approx 30\,\text{g}$, so $24\,\text{oz} \approx 24 \times 30 \approx 720\,\text{g}$

• • • TIP • • •

- Always check that your answers are sensible.

- Sometimes National Test questions use real-life situations:

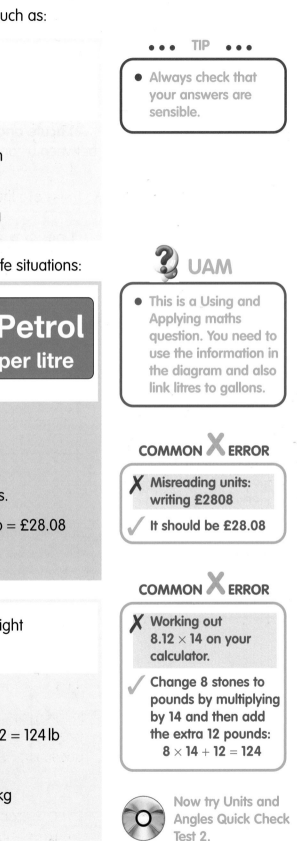

  2 Dylan needs 8 gallons of petrol to fill the tank in his car.

     About how much does he pay?

Petrol
78p per litre

? UAM

- This is a Using and Applying maths question. You need to use the information in the diagram and also link litres to gallons.

ANSWER

  2 This has to be done in two steps.

     Change 8 gallons into litres first:

     1 gallon $\approx 4\frac{1}{2}$ litres, so 8 gallons ≈ 36 litres.

     Now work out the cost: $36 \times 78p = 2808p = £28.08$

     He pays about £28.

COMMON ✗ ERROR

✗ Misreading units: writing £2808

✓ It should be £28.08

COMMON ✗ ERROR

✗ Working out 8.12×14 on your calculator.

✓ Change 8 stones to pounds by multiplying by 14 and then add the extra 12 pounds: $8 \times 14 + 12 = 124$

  3 Martha weighs 8 st 12 lb. Estimate her weight in kilograms.

ANSWER

  3 First change her weight into pounds:

     $8\,\text{st} = 8 \times 14 = 112\,\text{lb}$, so $8\,\text{st}\,12\,\text{lb} = 112 + 12 = 124\,\text{lb}$

     Now change 124 lb into kilograms:

     $1\,\text{kg} \approx 2\frac{1}{4}\,\text{lb}$, so $124\,\text{lb} \approx 124 \div 2.25 \approx 55.1\,\text{kg}$

     Martha weighs approximately 55 kg.

Now try Units and Angles Quick Check Test 2.

MEASURING AND DRAWING ANGLES

- acute angle
- obtuse angle
- right angle
- reflex angle

••• TIP •••

- The symbol for degrees is °, not %.

COMMON ✗ ERROR

✗ Reading the wrong angle on a semicircular protractor

✓ Always decide what type of angle you are measuring or drawing. Estimate angles first.

••• TIP •••

- A circular protractor is easier to use.

- Learn the names for the different types of angles:

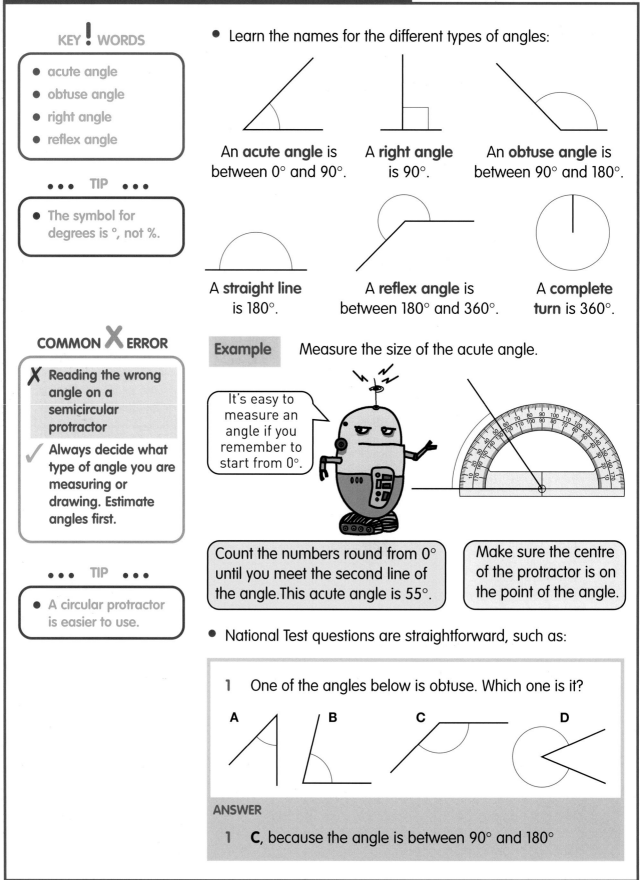

An **acute angle** is between 0° and 90°.

A **right angle** is 90°.

An **obtuse angle** is between 90° and 180°.

A **straight line** is 180°.

A **reflex angle** is between 180° and 360°.

A **complete turn** is 360°.

Example   Measure the size of the acute angle.

It's easy to measure an angle if you remember to start from 0°.

Count the numbers round from 0° until you meet the second line of the angle. This acute angle is 55°.

Make sure the centre of the protractor is on the point of the angle.

- National Test questions are straightforward, such as:

1   One of the angles below is obtuse. Which one is it?

A   B   C   D

ANSWER

1   **C**, because the angle is between 90° and 180°

- Sometimes National Test questions ask you to measure or draw an angle:

To draw an angle of 30°, draw a line: _____

Put the centre of the protractor on the end of the line. Mark off 30°:

30°

Take the protractor away. Join the points and label the angle:

30°

••• TIP •••
- Turn the page round until one of the lines of the angle is horizontal.

2   Measure the size of each of the following angles.

a

b

••• TIP •••
- To measure a reflex angle, measure the acute angle first and then subtract it from 360°, or use a circular protractor.

ANSWERS

2 a 47°   b 282°

3   Draw each of the following angles.

    a 30°   b 110°

••• TIP •••
- You will be expected to measure and draw angles to an accuracy of ± 2°.

ANSWERS

3 a   b

30°

110°

Now try Units and Angles Quick Check Test 3.

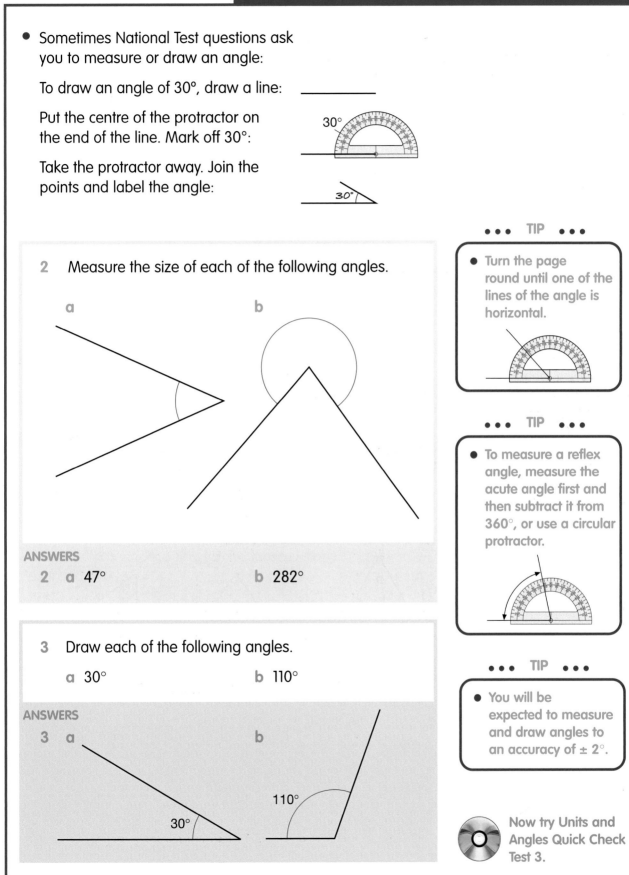

ANGLE FACTS

- exterior angle
- interior angle
- equilateral triangle
- isosceles triangle
- right-angled triangle

- You need to know how to use these five angle facts:

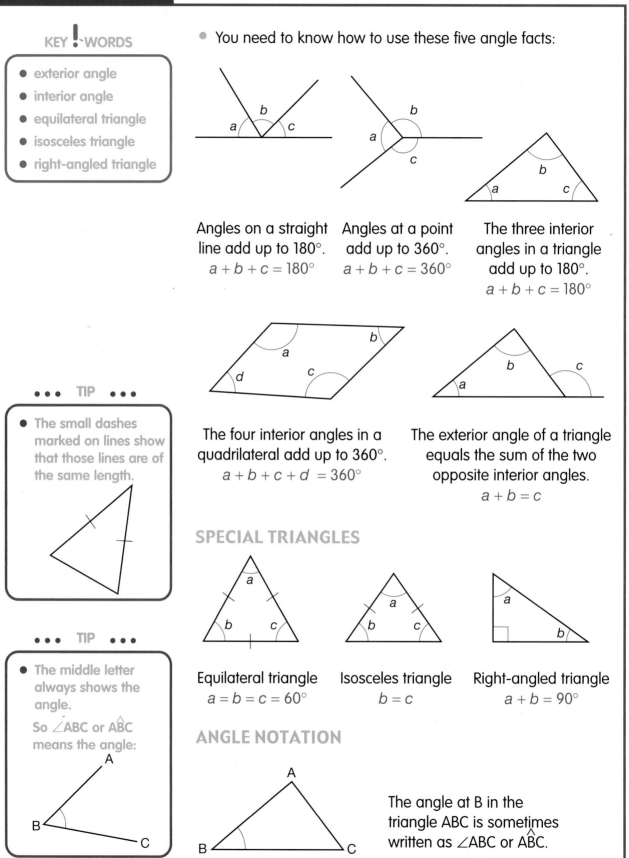

Angles on a straight line add up to 180°.
$$a + b + c = 180°$$

Angles at a point add up to 360°.
$$a + b + c = 360°$$

The three interior angles in a triangle add up to 180°.
$$a + b + c = 180°$$

The four interior angles in a quadrilateral add up to 360°.
$$a + b + c + d = 360°$$

The exterior angle of a triangle equals the sum of the two opposite interior angles.
$$a + b = c$$

SPECIAL TRIANGLES

Equilateral triangle
$$a = b = c = 60°$$

Isosceles triangle
$$b = c$$

Right-angled triangle
$$a + b = 90°$$

ANGLE NOTATION

The angle at B in the triangle ABC is sometimes written as $\angle ABC$ or $A\hat{B}C$.

... TIP ...

- The small dashes marked on lines show that those lines are of the same length.

... TIP ...

- The middle letter always shows the angle.
So $\angle ABC$ or $A\hat{B}C$ means the angle:

Example Find the angle marked x.

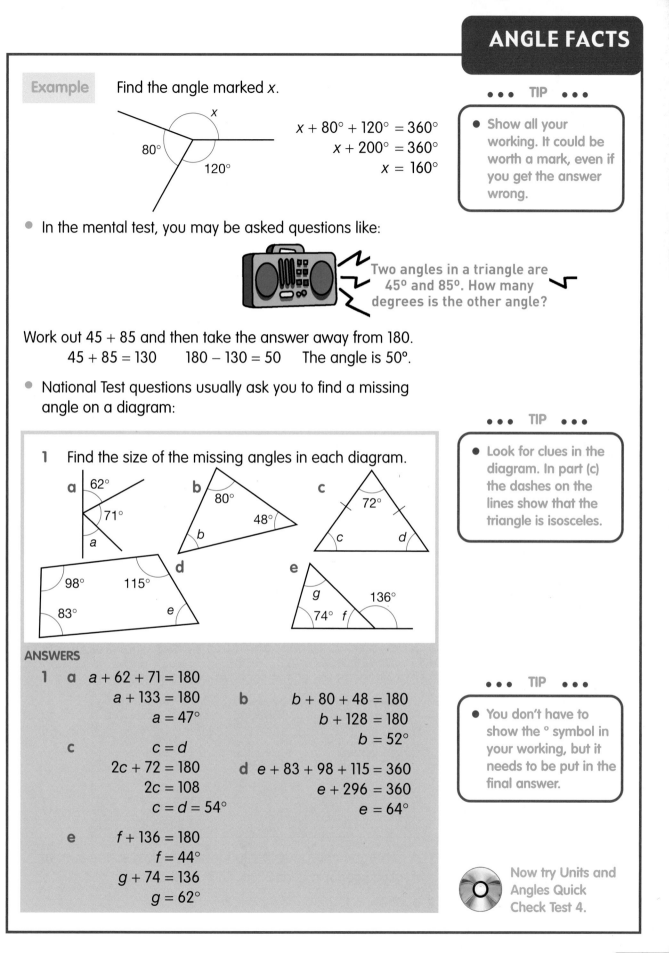

$$x + 80° + 120° = 360°$$
$$x + 200° = 360°$$
$$x = 160°$$

••• TIP •••

- Show all your working. It could be worth a mark, even if you get the answer wrong.

- In the mental test, you may be asked questions like:

Two angles in a triangle are 45° and 85°. How many degrees is the other angle?

Work out $45 + 85$ and then take the answer away from 180.

$$45 + 85 = 130 \qquad 180 - 130 = 50 \qquad \text{The angle is } 50°.$$

- National Test questions usually ask you to find a missing angle on a diagram:

••• TIP •••

- Look for clues in the diagram. In part (c) the dashes on the lines show that the triangle is isosceles.

1 Find the size of the missing angles in each diagram.

a 62° 71° a

b 80° 48° b

c 72° c d

d 98° 115° 83° e

e g 136° 74° f

ANSWERS

1 a $a + 62 + 71 = 180$
$a + 133 = 180$
$a = 47°$

b $b + 80 + 48 = 180$
$b + 128 = 180$
$b = 52°$

c $c = d$
$2c + 72 = 180$
$2c = 108$
$c = d = 54°$

d $e + 83 + 98 + 115 = 360$
$e + 296 = 360$
$e = 64°$

e $f + 136 = 180$
$f = 44°$
$g + 74 = 136$
$g = 62°$

••• TIP •••

- You don't have to show the ° symbol in your working, but it needs to be put in the final answer.

Now try Units and Angles Quick Check Test 4.

UNITS AND ANGLES

KEY ❗ WORDS

- vertically opposite angles
- alternate angles
- corresponding angles
- interior angles

● ● ● TIP ● ● ●

- Alternate angles: look for a 'Z'.
- Corresponding angles: look for a 'F'.
- Interior angles: look for a 'C'.

● ● ● TIP ● ● ●

- When solving angle problems, always give a reason for how you found each angle.
- Always use the correct mathematical words:
  - alternate angles
  - corresponding angles
  - interior angles

KEY ❗ WORDS

- polygon
- regular polygon
- pentagon
- hexagon
- heptagon
- octagon
- exterior angle

- Parallel lines never meet. They provide some special types of angles.

- You need to know these angle facts:

INTERSECTING LINES

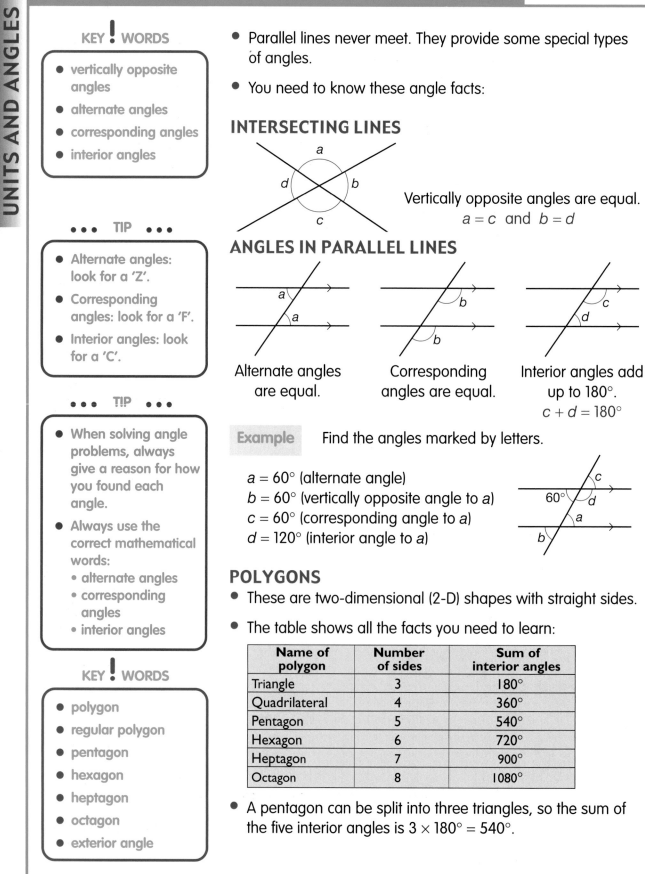

Vertically opposite angles are equal.
$a = c$ and $b = d$

ANGLES IN PARALLEL LINES

Alternate angles are equal.

Corresponding angles are equal.

Interior angles add up to 180°.
$c + d = 180°$

Example Find the angles marked by letters.

$a = 60°$ (alternate angle)
$b = 60°$ (vertically opposite angle to a)
$c = 60°$ (corresponding angle to a)
$d = 120°$ (interior angle to a)

POLYGONS

- These are two-dimensional (2-D) shapes with straight sides.

- The table shows all the facts you need to learn:

Name of polygon	Number of sides	Sum of interior angles
Triangle	3	180°
Quadrilateral	4	360°
Pentagon	5	540°
Hexagon	6	720°
Heptagon	7	900°
Octagon	8	1080°

- A pentagon can be split into three triangles, so the sum of the five interior angles is $3 \times 180° = 540°$.

REGULAR POLYGONS

- These are polygons with all sides equal and all angles equal.

- The regular pentagon has five equal interior angles and five equal exterior angles.
  Sum of 5 exterior angles = 360°
  So, each exterior angle = 72°
  Interior angle + exterior angle = 180°
  So, each interior angle = 108°

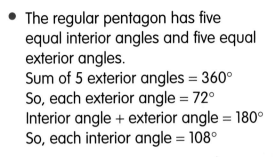

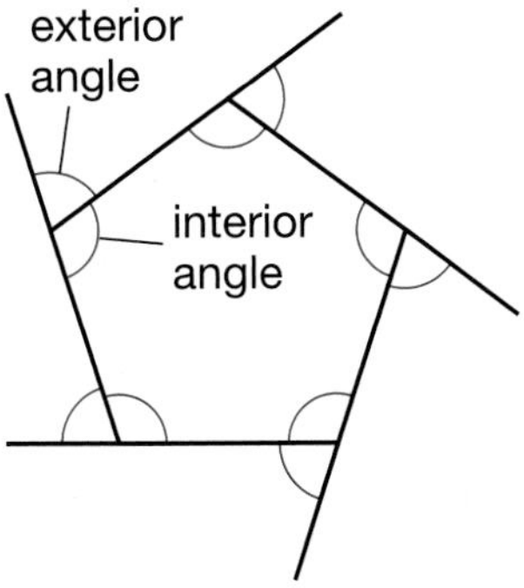

exterior angle

interior angle

- Typical National Test questions are:

COMMON ✗ ERROR

✗ interior angle + exterior angle = 360°

✓ The correct answer is:
interior angle + exterior angle = 180°.

---

1 ABCD is a rectangle.
Find the angles marked with a letter.

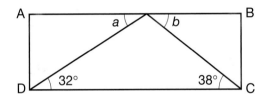

ANSWER

1 AB is parallel to CD, so $a = 32°$ (alternate angle)
and $b = 38°$ (alternate angle)

... TIP ...

- You can answer this question by using angles in a triangle:

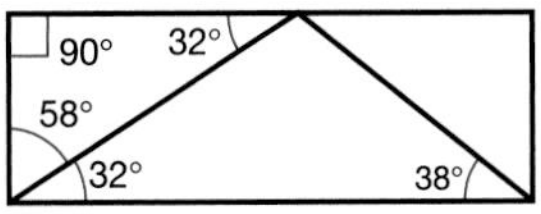

  90° 32°
  58°
  32°   38°

---

2 Find the size of the exterior angle and the interior angle of a regular hexagon.

ANSWER

2 Draw a diagram to help.

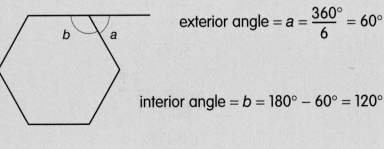

$$\text{exterior angle} = a = \frac{360°}{6} = 60°$$

$$\text{interior angle} = b = 180° - 60° = 120°$$

? UAM

- This is a Using and Applying maths question because there are other ways to do it.

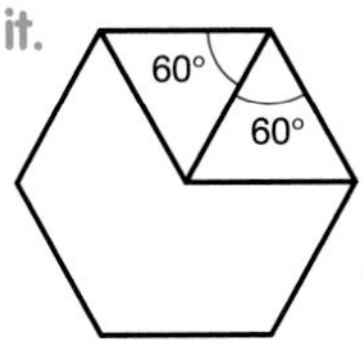

  60°
  60°

For example, you could split the hexagon into equilateral triangles.

Now try Units and Angles Quick Check Test 5.

Also try Units and Angles Final Test.

KEY ! WORDS

- reflection
- rotation
- line of symmetry
- order of rotational symmetry

... TIP ...

- You can use a mirror or tracing paper to check for a line of symmetry.

... TIP ...

- You can use tracing paper to check for rotational symmetry.

  You can ask for tracing paper in an exam.

... TIP ...

- Rotational symmetry of order 1 is the same as saying 'no rotational symmetry'. You can give either answer.

- There are two types of symmetry: reflective (line) symmetry and rotational symmetry.

REFLECTIVE SYMMETRY

- With reflective symmetry, you can draw a line across a shape and both halves will fold exactly together.

- The line is called a mirror line or a line of symmetry.

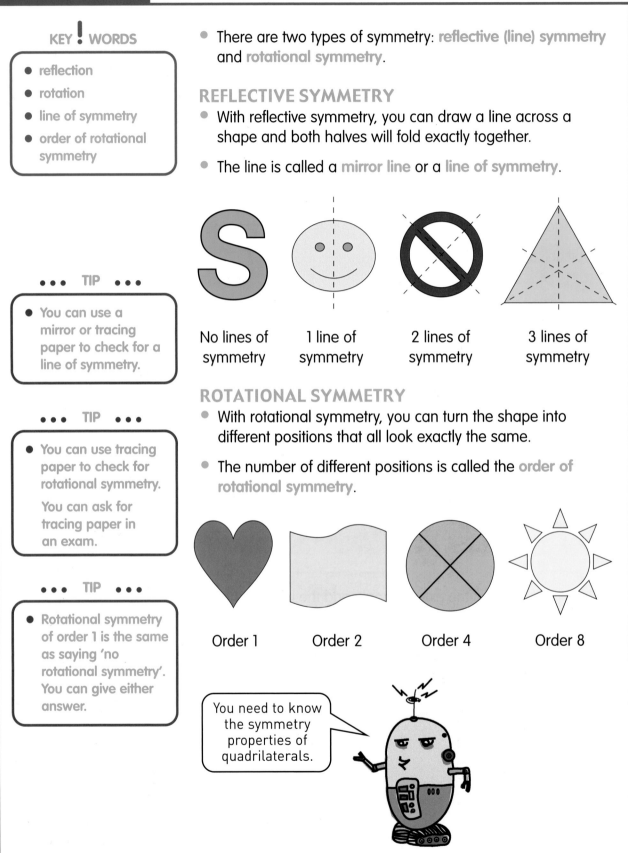

No lines of symmetry   1 line of symmetry   2 lines of symmetry   3 lines of symmetry

ROTATIONAL SYMMETRY

- With rotational symmetry, you can turn the shape into different positions that all look exactly the same.

- The number of different positions is called the order of rotational symmetry.

Order 1   Order 2   Order 4   Order 8

You need to know the symmetry properties of quadrilaterals.

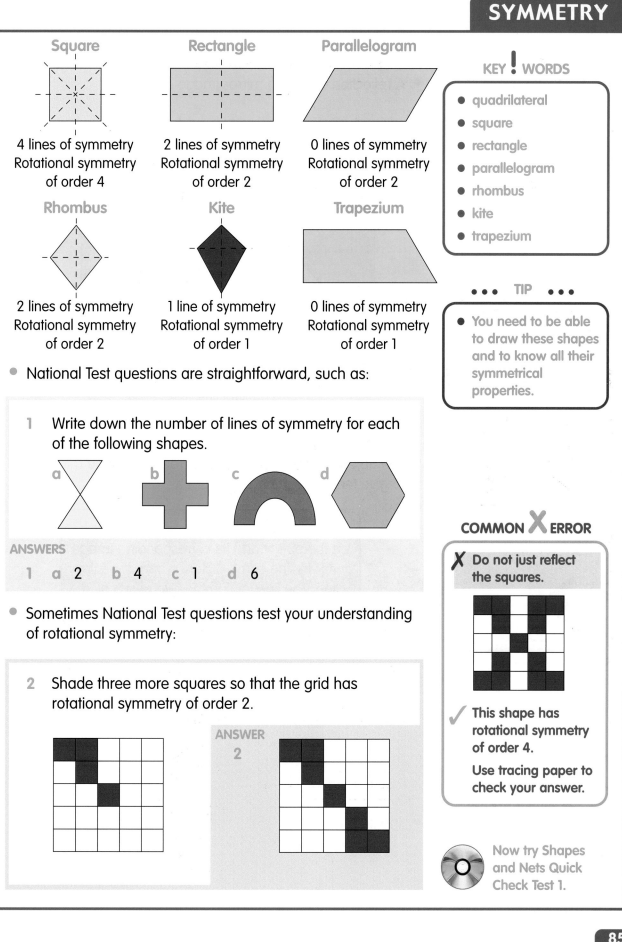

Square

4 lines of symmetry
Rotational symmetry
of order 4

Rectangle

2 lines of symmetry
Rotational symmetry
of order 2

Parallelogram

0 lines of symmetry
Rotational symmetry
of order 2

Rhombus

2 lines of symmetry
Rotational symmetry
of order 2

Kite

1 line of symmetry
Rotational symmetry
of order 1

Trapezium

0 lines of symmetry
Rotational symmetry
of order 1

KEY ! WORDS

- quadrilateral
- square
- rectangle
- parallelogram
- rhombus
- kite
- trapezium

• • • TIP • • •

- You need to be able to draw these shapes and to know all their symmetrical properties.

- National Test questions are straightforward, such as:

1 Write down the number of lines of symmetry for each of the following shapes.

a   b   c   d

ANSWERS

1 a 2   b 4   c 1   d 6

- Sometimes National Test questions test your understanding of rotational symmetry:

2 Shade three more squares so that the grid has rotational symmetry of order 2.

ANSWER
2

COMMON ✕ ERROR

✕ Do not just reflect the squares.

✓ This shape has rotational symmetry of order 4.

Use tracing paper to check your answer.

Now try Shapes and Nets Quick Check Test 1.

KEY ! WORDS

- reflection
- mirror line
- rotation
- angle of rotation
- centre of rotation
- object
- image

••• TIP •••

- If you trace the object and the image and fold along the mirror line,

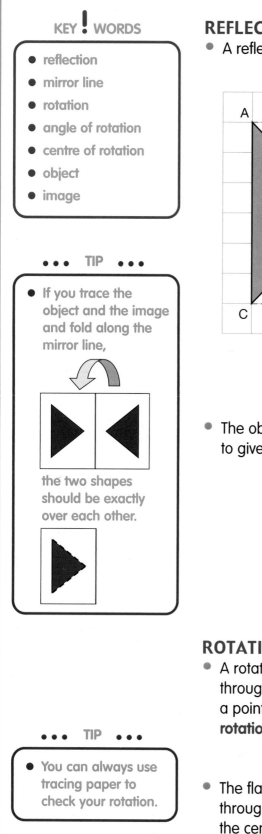

the two shapes should be exactly over each other.

REFLECTIONS

- A reflection creates a mirror image of a given object.

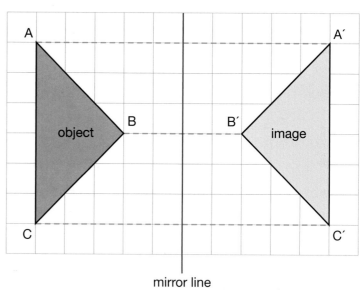

mirror line

- The object triangle ABC has been reflected in the mirror line to give the image triangle A'B'C'.

> The blue dashed lines show that any point on the object and its corresponding image point are the same distance from the mirror line. The line joining the two points also crosses the mirror line at right angles.

ROTATIONS

- A rotation turns the object through a given angle about a point called the **centre of rotation**.

••• TIP •••

- You can always use tracing paper to check your rotation.

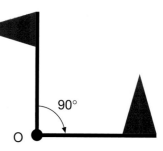

- The flag has been rotated through 90° clockwise about the centre of rotation O.

In both reflections and rotations, the object and the image are identical in their size and shape. We say that the two shapes are **congruent**.

KEY ! WORDS

● congruent

● National Test questions are straightforward, such as:

1 Rectangle A has been rotated onto rectangle B about the point O. Describe the rotation.

• • • TIP • • •

● Congruent means 'exactly the same shape and size'.
● Similar means 'the same shape but different sizes'.

ANSWER

1 Rectangle A can move clockwise or anti-clockwise, so there are two answers: a rotation of 90° anticlockwise or a rotation of 270° clockwise.

COMMON ✗ ERROR

✗ Confusing clockwise and anticlockwise.

✓ Clockwise is the direction the hands of a clock move.

● National Test questions may ask you to reflect a shape across a diagonal mirror line:

2 Reflect the triangle in the mirror line.

• • • TIP • • •

● Turn the page round so that the mirror line is horizontal or vertical.

This makes it much easier to see the reflection.

ANSWER

2

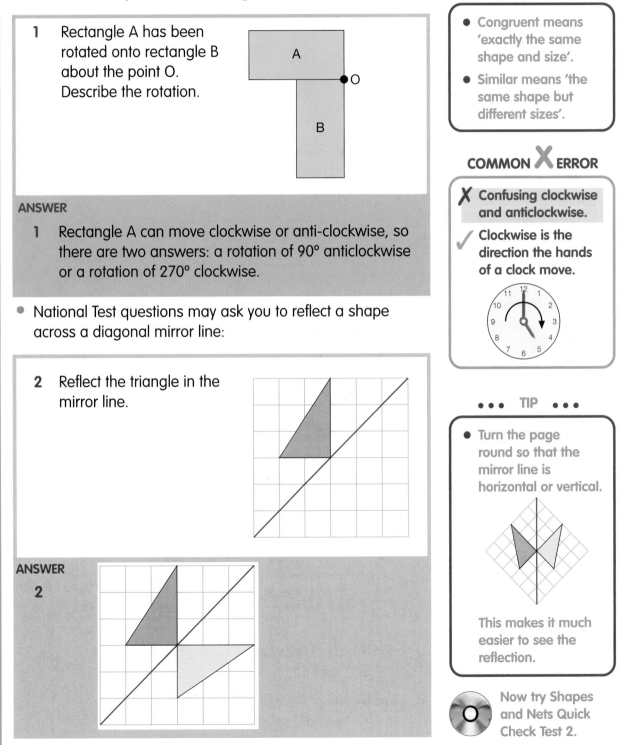

Now try Shapes and Nets Quick Check Test 2.

ENLARGEMENTS

KEY **!** WORDS

- enlargement
- centre of enlargement
- scale factor

- An **enlargement** changes the size of a shape.

- The **scale factor** tells you how many times bigger the shape is to be enlarged.

- To enlarge a shape, you also need a **centre of enlargement**.

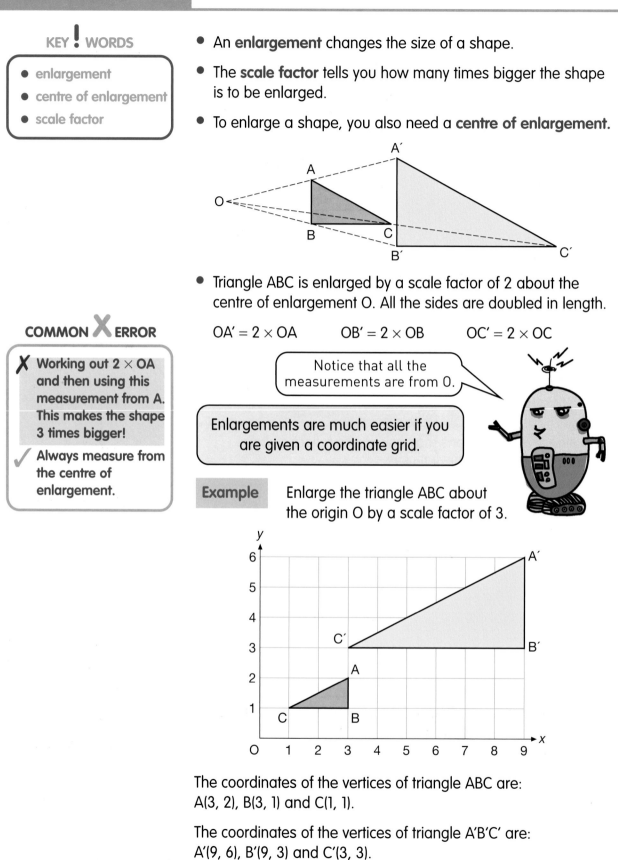

- Triangle ABC is enlarged by a scale factor of 2 about the centre of enlargement O. All the sides are doubled in length.

$$OA' = 2 \times OA \qquad OB' = 2 \times OB \qquad OC' = 2 \times OC$$

COMMON **✗** ERROR

✗ Working out 2 × OA and then using this measurement from A. This makes the shape 3 times bigger!

✓ Always measure from the centre of enlargement.

Notice that all the measurements are from O.

Enlargements are much easier if you are given a coordinate grid.

Example Enlarge the triangle ABC about the origin O by a scale factor of 3.

The coordinates of the vertices of triangle ABC are:
A(3, 2), B(3, 1) and C(1, 1).

The coordinates of the vertices of triangle A'B'C' are:
A'(9, 6), B'(9, 3) and C'(3, 3).

- A **vertex** is a corner of a shape. The plural is **vertices**.

- In the example on page 88, the coordinates of the vertices of triangle ABC are multiplied by the scale factor to give the vertices of triangle A'B'C'. This method works if the centre of enlargement is at the origin but not if it is elsewhere.

- National Test questions on enlargements are straightforward and generally only use a scale factor of 2:

1   Enlarge the trapezium ABCD by a scale factor of 2 about the origin O.

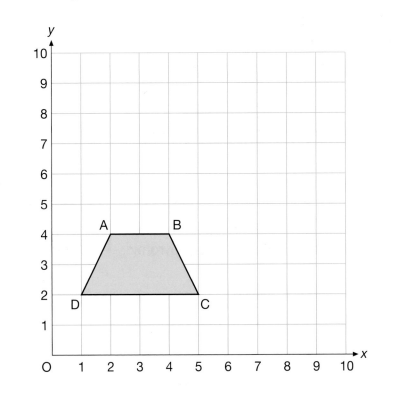

... TIP ...

- You can do this in two ways:

  Count squares
  D is 1 square across and 2 squares up so if it enlarged by a factor of 2, D' will be 2 squares across and 4 squares up.

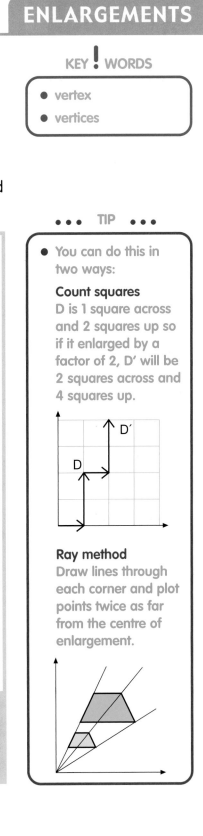

  Ray method
  Draw lines through each corner and plot points twice as far from the centre of enlargement.

ANSWER

1   The coordinates of the enlarged trapezium A'B'C'D' are:
A'(4, 8), B'(8, 8), C'(10, 4) and D'(2, 4).

Now try Shapes and Nets Quick Check Test 3.

3-D SHAPES

- 2-D shapes are called **polygons** and 3-D shapes are called **polyhedra**.

- These are the names of the 3-D shapes you need to know.

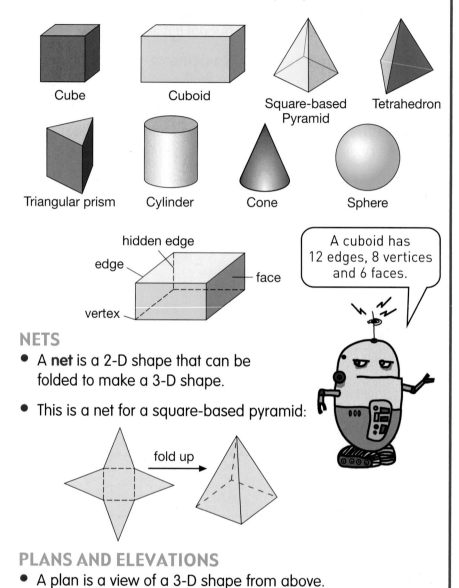

Cube   Cuboid   Square-based Pyramid   Tetrahedron

Triangular prism   Cylinder   Cone   Sphere

hidden edge

edge

face

vertex

A cuboid has 12 edges, 8 vertices and 6 faces.

NETS

- A **net** is a 2-D shape that can be folded to make a 3-D shape.

- This is a net for a square-based pyramid:

fold up

PLANS AND ELEVATIONS

- A plan is a view of a 3-D shape from above.

- An elevation is a view of a 3-D shape from one side.

- These are the views for a triangular prism:

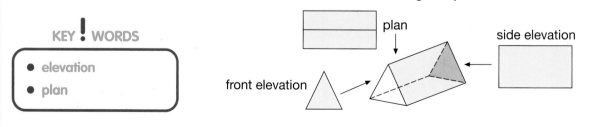

plan

side elevation

front elevation

ISOMETRIC DRAWINGS

- 3-D shapes drawn on isometric paper are more accurate, and measurements can be taken from the diagram.

- This is the isometric drawing for a cuboid:

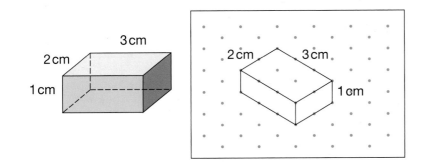

PLANES OF SYMMETRY

- A 3-D shape has **plane symmetry** if it can be cut in half so that one half is a mirror image of the other half.

- A cuboid has three planes of symmetry:

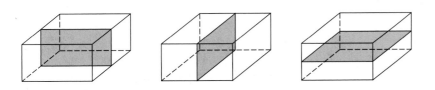

- National Test questions are straightforward, such as:

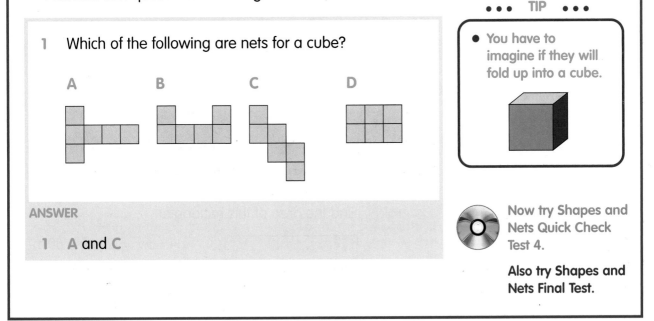

1   Which of the following are nets for a cube?

A   B   C   D

ANSWER

1   A and C

● ● ●   TIP   ● ● ●

- You have to imagine if they will fold up into a cube.

Now try Shapes and Nets Quick Check Test 4.

Also try Shapes and Nets Final Test.

PERIMETER AND AREA

... TIP ...

- When finding a perimeter, put a mark on one vertex and count round the sides until you get back to the start.

COMMON ✗ ERROR

✗ Confusing perimeter and area

✓ Perimeter is the distance round the outside of a shape. Area is the space inside it.

COMMON ✗ ERROR

✗ Writing the units as m or missing out the units

✓ Some Test questions have a mark for correct units.

... TIP ...

- It is quicker to write down the formula using letters.

PERIMETER

- This is the total distance around the outside of a 2-D shape.

Example Find the perimeter of this shape.

The perimeter is
6 + 3 + 4 + 2 + 10 + 5
= 30 cm.

6 cm

5 cm

2 cm

10 cm

AREA

- This is the amount of space inside a 2-D shape.

Remember the common units for area are: mm^2, cm^2 or m^2.

AREA BY COUNTING SQUARES

Example Estimate the area of this shape.

	x	x	x	x	x	
x	1	2	3	4	x
x	5	6	7	8	x

First count the number of whole squares. Then mark the squares where the area is more than half a square.

So an estimate for the area is $8 + 9 \times \frac{1}{2} = 12\frac{1}{2}$ cm^2.

AREA OF A RECTANGLE

- Area = length × width
    $A = l \times w$
    $A = lw$

width

length

Example Find the area of this rectangle:

$A = lw = 12 \times 5 = 60\,m^2$

5 m

12 m

AREA FORMULAE

- In these formulae, *b* stands for 'base' and *h* stands for 'height' although the correct term is 'perpendicular height'.

Parallelogram

$A = bh$

Triangle

$A = \dfrac{bh}{2}$

Trapezium

$A = \dfrac{(a + b)h}{2}$

••• TIP •••

- Do not try to work these out in your head. Always substitute numbers into the formula. You will have more chance of reaching the correct answer.

Example   Find the area of these shapes.

a

3 cm

10 cm

b

5 cm

4 cm

9 cm

a $A = \dfrac{bh}{2} = \dfrac{10 \times 3}{2}$

$= 15 \text{ cm}^2$

b $A = \dfrac{(a + b)h}{2} = \dfrac{(9 + 5) \times 4}{2}$

$= 28 \text{ cm}^2$

- In the mental test you will be expected to answer questions such as:

A square has an area of 36 cm². What is the perimeter of the square?

••• TIP •••

- Do not just divide 36 by 4. First use square root to find the side, √36 = 6, and then multiply by 4 to find the perimeter.

The length of a side of the square is 6 cm, since 6 × 6 = 36. So the perimeter of the square is 4 × 6 = 24 cm.

- A typical National Test question is:

1   On a grid, draw a triangle that has an area of 6 cm².

ANSWER

1   Possible triangles are:

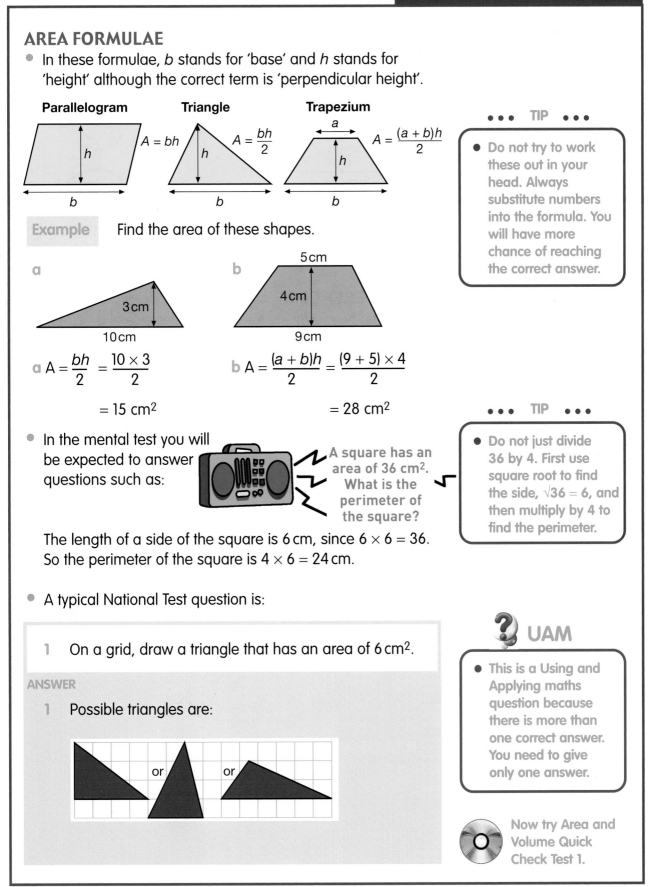

or   or

? UAM

- This is a Using and Applying maths question because there is more than one correct answer. You need to give only one answer.

Now try Area and Volume Quick Check Test 1.

CIRCUMFERENCE AND AREA OF A CIRCLE

KEY ! WORDS

- diameter
- radius
- circumference
- π

- These are the names of the different parts of a circle.

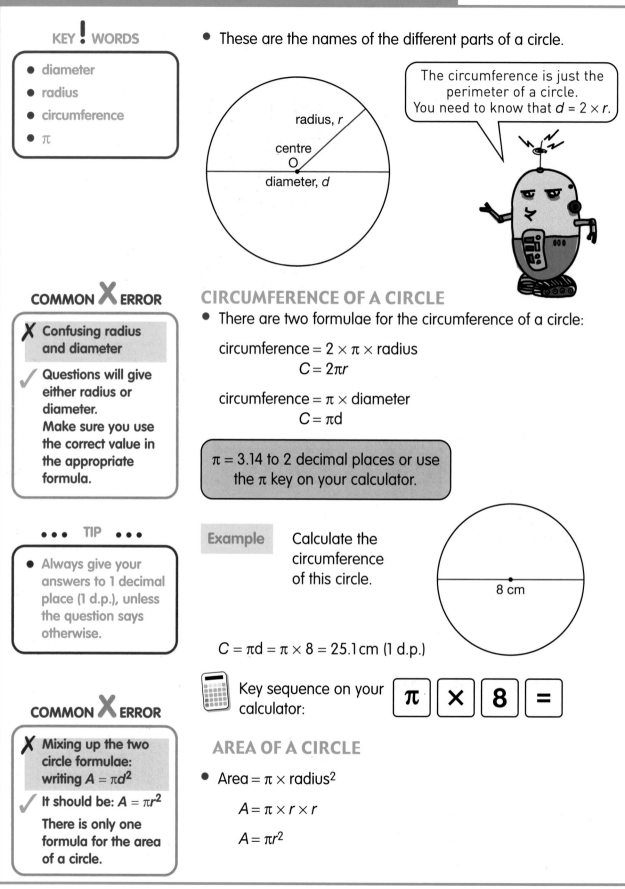

radius, r

centre O

diameter, d

The circumference is just the perimeter of a circle. You need to know that $d = 2 \times r$.

COMMON ✗ ERROR

✗ **Confusing radius and diameter**

✓ Questions will give either radius or diameter.
Make sure you use the correct value in the appropriate formula.

CIRCUMFERENCE OF A CIRCLE

- There are two formulae for the circumference of a circle:

circumference $= 2 \times \pi \times$ radius
$$C = 2\pi r$$

circumference $= \pi \times$ diameter
$$C = \pi d$$

$\pi = 3.14$ to 2 decimal places or use the π key on your calculator.

... TIP ...

- Always give your answers to 1 decimal place (1 d.p.), unless the question says otherwise.

Example   Calculate the circumference of this circle.

8 cm

$C = \pi d = \pi \times 8 = 25.1$ cm (1 d.p.)

Key sequence on your calculator:

$\boxed{\pi}$ $\boxed{\times}$ $\boxed{8}$ $\boxed{=}$

COMMON ✗ ERROR

✗ Mixing up the two circle formulae: writing $A = \pi d^2$

✓ It should be: $A = \pi r^2$
There is only one formula for the area of a circle.

AREA OF A CIRCLE

- Area $= \pi \times$ radius^2

$$A = \pi \times r \times r$$

$$A = \pi r^2$$

Example Calculate the area of this circle.

Write down the formula first and always show your working.

7 cm

$A = \pi r^2 = \pi \times 7^2 = 153.9 \text{ cm}^2$ (1 d.p.)

Key sequence on your calculator: | π | $\times$ | 7 | x^2 | = |

• National Test questions are straightforward, such as:

1 Mark's bike wheel has a radius of 30 cm.
   Calculate its circumference, giving your answer to the nearest centimetre.

ANSWERS

1 Here $r = 30$ cm, so $d = 60$ cm.
   $C = \pi d = \pi \times 60 = 188$ cm (nearest cm)

• Sometimes National Test questions may be more complex:

2 The circle and the square have the same area.

4 cm

x

Calculate x, the length of the side of the square.

ANSWERS

2 The area of the circle is $A = \pi r^2 = \pi \times 4^2 = 50.26\ldots$
   So $x = \sqrt{50.26\ldots} = 7.1$ cm (1 d.p.)

••• TIP •••

• Remember to include the correct units with your answer.

? UAM

• This is a Using and Applying maths question because you have to decide on a strategy and link the formulae for area of a circle and a square.

••• TIP •••

• Use the square root key of your calculator to work out the square root of the display.

Now try Area and Volume Quick Check Test 2.

VOLUME

KEY ! WORDS

- volume
- capacity
- litre

VOLUME

- Volume is the amount of space inside a 3-D shape.

> Remember the common units for volume are: mm^3, cm^3 or m^3.

... TIP ...

- It is quicker to write the formula using letters.

VOLUME OF A CUBOID

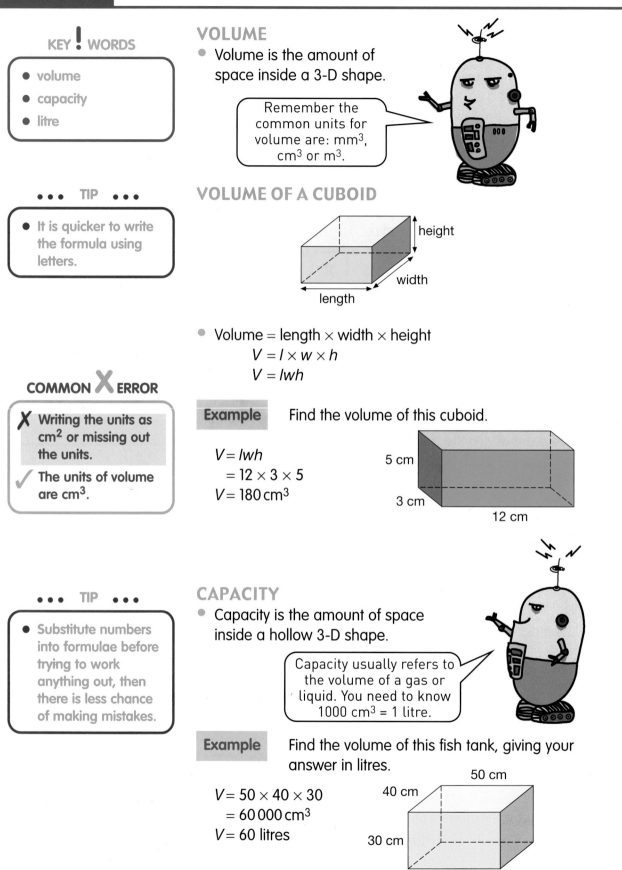

height

width

length

- Volume = length × width × height

$$V = l \times w \times h$$
$$V = lwh$$

COMMON ✗ ERROR

✗ Writing the units as cm^2 or missing out the units.

✓ The units of volume are cm^3.

Example   Find the volume of this cuboid.

$V = lwh$
$\quad = 12 \times 3 \times 5$
$V = 180\,cm^3$

5 cm

3 cm

12 cm

... TIP ...

- Substitute numbers into formulae before trying to work anything out, then there is less chance of making mistakes.

CAPACITY

- Capacity is the amount of space inside a hollow 3-D shape.

> Capacity usually refers to the volume of a gas or liquid. You need to know $1000\,cm^3 = 1$ litre.

Example   Find the volume of this fish tank, giving your answer in litres.

$V = 50 \times 40 \times 30$
$\quad = 60\,000\,cm^3$
$V = 60$ litres

50 cm

40 cm

30 cm

- In the mental test you may be asked questions like:

The volume of a cube is 27 cm^3. What is the length of an edge of the cube?

Since $27 = 3 \times 3 \times 3$, the length of an edge $= 3$ cm.

- National Test questions are straightforward, such as:

1   This is a net of a cuboid. If one square has an area of 1 cm^2, what is the volume of the cuboid?

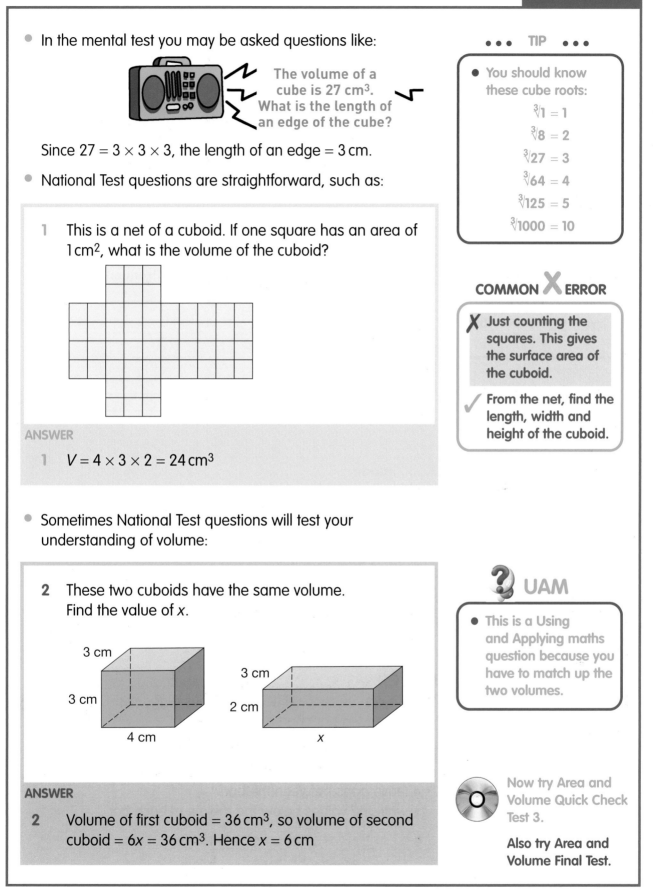

ANSWER

1   $V = 4 \times 3 \times 2 = 24$ cm^3

COMMON ✗ ERROR

✗ Just counting the squares. This gives the surface area of the cuboid.

✓ From the net, find the length, width and height of the cuboid.

- Sometimes National Test questions will test your understanding of volume:

2   These two cuboids have the same volume. Find the value of x.

3 cm
3 cm
4 cm

3 cm
2 cm
x

ANSWER

2   Volume of first cuboid $= 36$ cm^3, so volume of second cuboid $= 6x = 36$ cm^3. Hence $x = 6$ cm

❓ UAM

- This is a Using and Applying maths question because you have to match up the two volumes.

Now try Area and Volume Quick Check Test 3.

Also try Area and Volume Final Test.

FREQUENCY TABLES

KEY ! WORDS

- data
- survey
- questionnaire
- tally chart
- frequency table

- Statistics is the study of data and showing it in tables and diagrams.

- Statistics involves collecting and interpreting data.

- Data is best collected by carrying out **surveys** or by using **questionnaires**.

- Data can be sorted easily by putting it into a table called a **tally chart** or a **frequency table**.

  This frequency table shows the scores when a dice has been thrown 30 times.

Score	Tally	Frequency
1	⌕⌕⌕ I	6
2	⌕⌕⌕	5
3	I I I	3
4	⌕⌕⌕ I I	7
5	⌕⌕⌕	5
6	I I I I	4
	Total	30

... TIP ...

- Always check that your frequencies add up to the total.

MODE AND RANGE

- The **mode** for a set of data is the value that occurs most often.

  From the frequency table above, the score that occurs most often is 4. So we say the mode of the scores is 4 or the modal score is 4.

- The **range** for a set of data is calculated as:
  the highest value – the lowest value

  From the frequency table, the range of the scores is $6 - 1 = 5$.

COMMON ✗ ERROR

✗ Picking the largest frequency as the mode.

✓ The mode is the value with highest frequency.

BAR CHARTS

- Data can be represented on various diagrams. One easy way is to draw a bar chart for the data.

- When drawing a bar chart always remember to:
  - label the axes
  - leave gaps between the bars
  - write the values below the middle of each bar.

KEY ! WORDS

- bar chart
- mode
- range
- discrete data

This bar chart shows the scores on the dice for the frequency table on the previous page.

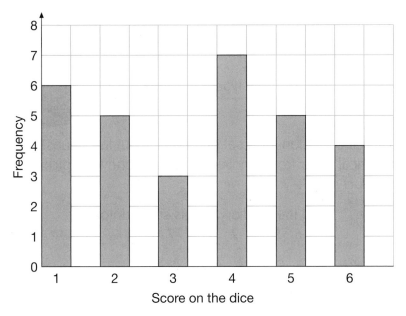

- National Test questions are straightforward, such as:

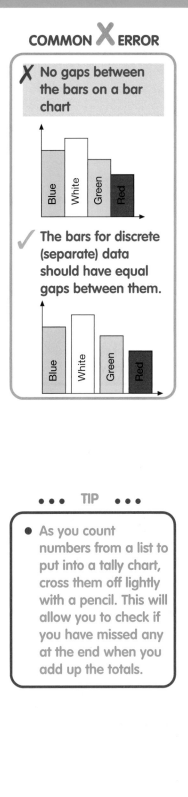

✗ **No gaps between the bars on a bar chart**

Blue White Green Red

✓ **The bars for discrete (separate) data should have equal gaps between them.**

Blue White Green Red

---

1 Here are the numbers of goals scored by a team in 20 games.

0 1 0 1 1 2 1 3 2 4
0 1 3 4 2 0 1 1 0 2

a Draw a frequency table to show the scores.

b What is the mode for the number of goals scored?

c What is the range of the number of goals scored?

● ● ● **TIP** ● ● ●

- As you count numbers from a list to put into a tally chart, cross them off lightly with a pencil. This will allow you to check if you have missed any at the end when you add up the totals.

ANSWERS

1 a

Score	Tally	Frequency
0	ⱵⱵⱵ	5
1	ⱵⱵⱵ ‖	7
2	‖‖‖	4
3	‖	2
4	‖	2
	Total	20

b The mode is 1 goal.

c The range is 4 – 0 = 4 goals

Now try Averages and Range Quick Check Test 1.

KEY **!** WORDS

- median
- mean

- An **average** is a typical value for a set of data.

  You have already met one average – the **mode**.

  Two others are the **median** and the **mean**.

  > Make sure you know the difference between the three types of average.

THE MEDIAN

- To find the median for a set of data, first put the values in numerical order from smallest to largest, and then pick out the exact middle value.

... TIP ...

- Cross off from the two ends to find the middle value.

Example   Find the median for this set of data.

6 5 9 2 6 4 7 8 3

In order: 2̶ 3̶ 4̶ 5̶ 6 6̶ 7̶ 8̶ 9̶
The median is 6.

Example   The ages of six people are:
21, 32, 25, 19, 23 and 18.
Find their median age.

In order: 1̶8̶ 1̶9̶ 21 23 2̶5̶ 3̶2̶

There are two numbers in the middle, so the median is the number halfway between 21 and 23. The median is 22.

COMMON ✗ ERROR

✗ Not putting the data in numerical order.

✓ If data is not in order, it must be put in order.

THE MEAN

- The mean is the average that is commonly used.

- To find the mean for a set of data, first find the total of all the values and then divide this total by the number of values.

  The symbol for the mean is $\bar{x}$.

$$\bar{x} = \frac{\text{Total of all values}}{\text{Number of values}}$$

... TIP ...

- MOde = MOst common

  Median = Medium (middle)

  Mean = the 'nastiest' because it is the hardest to work out.

Example   The ages of six people are:
21, 32, 25, 19, 23 and 18.

Find their mean age.

$$\bar{x} = \frac{\text{Total of all values}}{\text{Number of values}} = \frac{138}{6} = 23$$

THE MEAN FROM A FREQUENCY TABLE

- To find the mean from a frequency table, add an extra column to find the total of all the values.

COMMON ✗ ERROR

✗ $6 \times 0 = 6$
✓ $6 \times 0 = 0$
anything $\times 0 = 0$!

Example: The frequency table shows the marks for 20 pupils in a spelling test. Find the mean mark.

Mark, x	Frequency, f	$x \times f$
5	1	5
6	0	0
7	3	21
8	5	40
9	8	72
10	3	30
Totals	20	168

$$\bar{x} = \frac{\text{Total of all values}}{\text{Number of values}} = \frac{168}{20} = 8.4$$

••• TIP •••

- If the mean is not an exact answer, then round it to 1 decimal place.

- In the mental test you will be expected to answer questions such as:

What is the mean of 19, 21, 23 and 37?

••• TIP •••

- $19 + 21 = 40$ and $23 + 37 = 60$
So $40 + 60 = 100$.

In mental tests, the numbers will always be easy to add up.

Add the numbers together: $19 + 21 + 23 + 37 = 100$
$\bar{x} = 100 \div 4 = 25$

- Typical National Test questions are:

1 a Find the mean of the numbers on these cards.

3 4 6 7

b Another card is added and the mean goes up by 2.

3 4 6 7 ?

What number is on the new card?

••• TIP •••

- Always check that your answer is sensible. The mean will always be between the lowest and highest values. Usually it will be about half way between them.

ANSWERS

1 a The mean $= (3 + 4 + 6 + 7) \div 4 = 20 \div 4 = 5$

b The new mean is 7, so the five numbers add up to 35.
The number on the new card is $35 - 20 = 15$.

Now try Averages and Range Quick Check Test 2.

AVERAGES AND RANGE

KEY **!** WORDS

KEY **!** WORDS

- grouped data
- frequency diagram
- frequency polygon
- continuous data

- When there is a lot of data covering a wide range, you may collect it using groups.

This table shows the marks for Year 11 in their mathematics mock exam.

Mark, m	Frequency, f
$20 < m \leq 30$	7
$30 < m \leq 40$	29
$40 < m \leq 50$	56
$50 < m \leq 60$	32
$60 < m \leq 70$	15
$70 < m \leq 80$	8
$80 < m \leq 90$	3

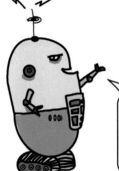

$20 < m \leq 30$ means marks that are bigger than 20 and less than, or equal to, 30.

••• TIP •••

- Because this is continuous data, the bars can be joined together.

- If you add up all the frequencies, you can tell that 150 pupils took the examination.

- However, you cannot tell exactly what any of the following are:
  the lowest mark, the highest mark, the mode, the median, the range or the exact mean.

- A **frequency diagram** can be used to show the shape of the distribution.

••• TIP •••

- As the marks start at 20, you could start the mark axis:

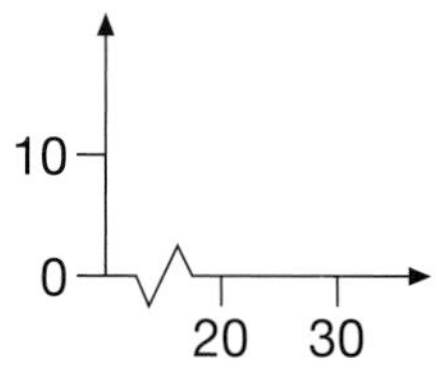

This means there is no data below 20.

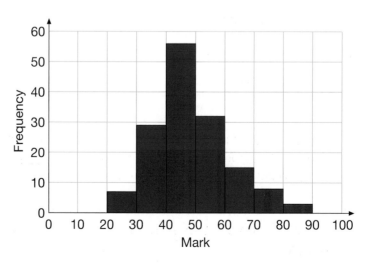

Example

30 pupils took a ten-question mental arithmetic test. These are the results.

2 3 5 3 6 1 3 7 8 9 10 8 7 7 4
6 5 4 1 3 5 3 8 9 10 3 2 1 6 4

Collect the data into a grouped table using groups:
$1 < x \leq 2$, $3 < x \leq 4$, and so on.

First decide what the groups will be. The biggest group will be $9 < x \leq 10$. Then count the data using tallies.

Mark	Tally	Frequency
$1 < x \leq 2$	⊦⊦⊦⊦	5
$3 < x \leq 4$	⊦⊦⊦⊦ IIII	9
$5 < x \leq 6$	⊦⊦⊦⊦ I	6
$7 < x \leq 8$	⊦⊦⊦⊦ I	6
$9 < x \leq 10$	IIII	4
	Total	30

• A typical National Test question is:

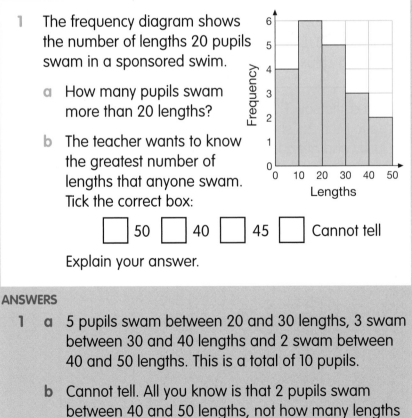

1 The frequency diagram shows the number of lengths 20 pupils swam in a sponsored swim.

   a How many pupils swam more than 20 lengths?

   b The teacher wants to know the greatest number of lengths that anyone swam. Tick the correct box:

     ☐ 50 ☐ 40 ☐ 45 ☐ Cannot tell

   Explain your answer.

ANSWERS

1 a 5 pupils swam between 20 and 30 lengths, 3 swam between 30 and 40 lengths and 2 swam between 40 and 50 lengths. This is a total of 10 pupils.

   b Cannot tell. All you know is that 2 pupils swam between 40 and 50 lengths, not how many lengths they swam.

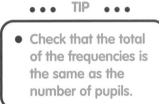
 Now try Averages and Range Quick Check Test 3.

COMPARING DISTRIBUTIONS

- range
- mean
- median
- mean
- consistent

- You compare distributions in everyday situations, without even realising it.

Example   Two dinner ladies, Mary and Doris, serve chips in the school canteen. Rajid went to Mary for his chips for a week. Mary gave out 18, 23, 25, 25, 34 chips.

The following week Rajid went to Doris for his chips. Doris gave out 23, 25, 27, 25, 25 chips.
Which dinner lady should Rajid go to to be given the most chips?

First, look at the averages and range:

	Mean	Median	Mode	Range
Mary	25	25	25	16
Doris	25	25	25	2

• • •   TIP   • • •

- The range measures the spread of the data so gives an indication of how **consistent** the data is.

The averages are the same but Mary's range is much larger than Doris'. So if Rajid caught Mary on a good day, he may have as many as 34 chips, but on a bad day he may have as few as 18. Doris is very consistent and will always give about 25 chips.

• • •   TIP   • • •

- When comparing data using ranges and averages, you must refer to them both in your answer.

You could say 'The averages are the same' and 'I would go to Mary as she has a bigger range and you might be lucky and get a lot of chips' or you could say 'I would go to Doris as she has a smaller range and is more consistent'. It doesn't matter who you chose as long as you mention the average and the range and give reasons for your choice.

- In the mental test, you may be asked questions like:

Give three numbers with a mode of 5 and a range of 2.

If there are three numbers and 5 is the mode, then two of the numbers must be 5. To give a range of 2, the other number must be 3 or 7.
So there are two answers: 3, 5, 5 or 5, 5, 7.

● Typical National Test questions are:

... TIP ...

● Compare the averages, even if they are the same. Also compare the ranges.

1 John records the lateness of two school buses A and B.
   Over a week, bus A is 0, 2, 5, 7 and 1 minute late.
   Over the same week, bus B is 2, 4, 2, 4, 3 minutes late.

   a Work out the mean and range for bus A.

   b Work out the mean and range for bus B.

   c Which bus is the more reliable?
      Give reasons for your answer.

... TIP ...

● Compare the averages, even if they are the same. Also compare the ranges.

ANSWERS

1 a Mean = $(0 + 2 + 5 + 7 + 1) \div 5 = 15 \div 5 = 3$ minutes
      Range = $7 - 0 = 7$ minutes

   b Mean = $(2 + 4 + 2 + 4 + 3) \div 5 = 15 \div 5 = 3$ minutes
      Range = $4 - 2 = 2$ minutes

   c Both buses have the same mean but bus B has a
      smaller range so is the more consistent. Bus B is
      more reliable even though it is always late.

2 Jayne needs to pick an attacker for the netball team.
   She looks at the scoring record of Asha and Rhoda.
   In Asha's last five matches she scored 5, 7, 2, 9, 2 goals.
   In Rhoda's last five matches she scored 5, 6, 5, 4, 5
   goals.
   Who should Jayne choose and why?

UAM

● This is a Using and Applying maths question. You have to decide which average to use.

ANSWER

2 The averages for Asha are: Mode 2, Median 5, Mean 5
   The averages for Rhoda are: Mode 5, Median 5, Mean 5
   The range of Asha's scores is $9 - 2 = 7$
   The range of Rhoda's scores is $6 - 4 = 2$
   The averages are the same, except for modes, but
   Rhoda has a smaller range so she is more consistent.
   Although Asha may get a high score, she may also get
   a low score, so Jayne should pick Rhoda.

Now try Averages and Range Quick Check Test 4.

Also try Averages and Range Final Test.

KEY ❗ WORDS

- line graph
- time series
- trend line
- distribution

- A **line graph** is a clear way of showing changes in data.

  The maximum temperature in a town each month for a year is recorded.

Jan	Feb	Mar	Apr	May	Jun	Jul	Aug	Sep	Oct	Nov	Dec
4	9	13	19	25	28	32	29	22	17	13	7

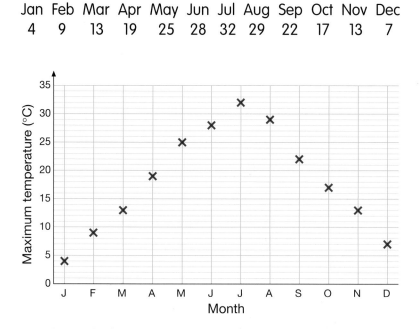

- You can see from the graph that the temperature rises in summer. If we join the points, the lines between them have no meaning but they show the trend of the temperatures over the year.

COMMON ✘ ERROR

✘ Reading values from trend lines

✓ The lines are drawn just to show the shape of the distribution. The maximum temperature halfway between January and February has no meaning anyway.

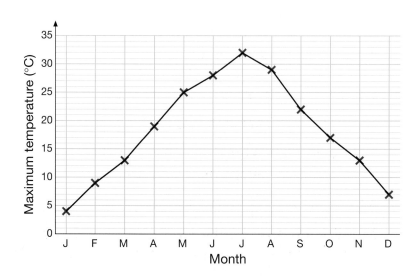

Example The following graph shows the monthly gas use for the Jones family.

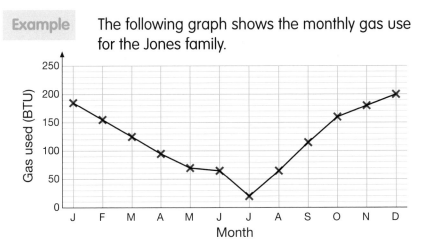

 UAM

- This is a Using and Applying maths question. You have to realise that the sharp drop in July means a lot less gas is used, and relate this to the family being on holiday.

a   During which month was the most gas used?

b   During one of the months in the summer the Jones family went on holiday. Which month was this? Give a reason for your answer.

The answers are:

a   The most gas was used during December as this was the highest value on the graph.

b   July. The amount of gas drops a lot in July suggesting that the family were not at home.

- A typical National Test question is:

1 Jason records the temperature in his greenhouse once an hour. At 8 a.m. it was 14 °C, at 9 a.m. it was 20 °C, at 10 a.m. it was 25 °C and at 11 a.m. it was 29 °C. This information is shown on the graph.

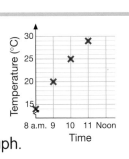

a   Estimate the temperature at 10.30 a.m.

b   Explain why the graph cannot be used to predict the temperature at 12 noon.

ANSWERS

1   a   Using the trend line between 10 a.m. and 11 a.m. the temperature can be estimated as 27 °C.

   b   The trend line may not continue after 11 a.m. The sun could go in, or the windows could be opened.

••• **TIP** •••

- You can estimate values from trend lines but you cannot say for sure what the values are.

 Now try Statistical Representation Quick Check Test 1.

PIE CHARTS

• • • TIP • • •

- Always label pie charts and give a title to show what the pie chart represents.

• • • TIP • • •

- It is useful to know the factors of 360:

  1×360 2×180

  3×120 4×90

  5×72 6×60

  8×45 9×40

  10×36 12×30

  15×24 18×20

• You need to be able to read and draw pie charts. The main fact to remember is that frequencies are represented by angles and that the total frequency is equivalent to 360°.

Example

Favourite colours of Form 7A

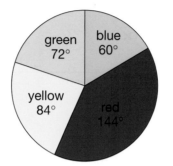

green 72°
blue 60°
yellow 84°
red 144°

This pie chart shows the favourite colours of Class 7A. If 5 pupils choose blue as their favourite colour, how many pupils are in Class 7A?

There are 5 pupils represented by 60°,
so 1 pupil is represented by 60° ÷ 5 = 12°.
There are 360° in the circle, and 360 ÷ 12 = 30.
There are 30 pupils in the class.

Example

This table shows the types of vehicles parked in a motorway service area.

Type of vehicle	Frequency
Car	40
Vans	22
Motorbikes	8
Lorries	20

Draw a pie chart to show the data.

First add up the frequencies: they total 90.
Divide this into 360 to find the angle that represents each vehicle: 360° ÷ 90 = 4°.
Now multiply each frequency by this figure. This is easily shown by adding another column to the table.

Type of vehicle	Frequency	Angle
Car	40	$40 \times 4 = 160°$
Vans	22	$22 \times 4 = 88°$
Motorbikes	8	$8 \times 4 = 32°$
Lorries	20	$20 \times 4 = 80°$

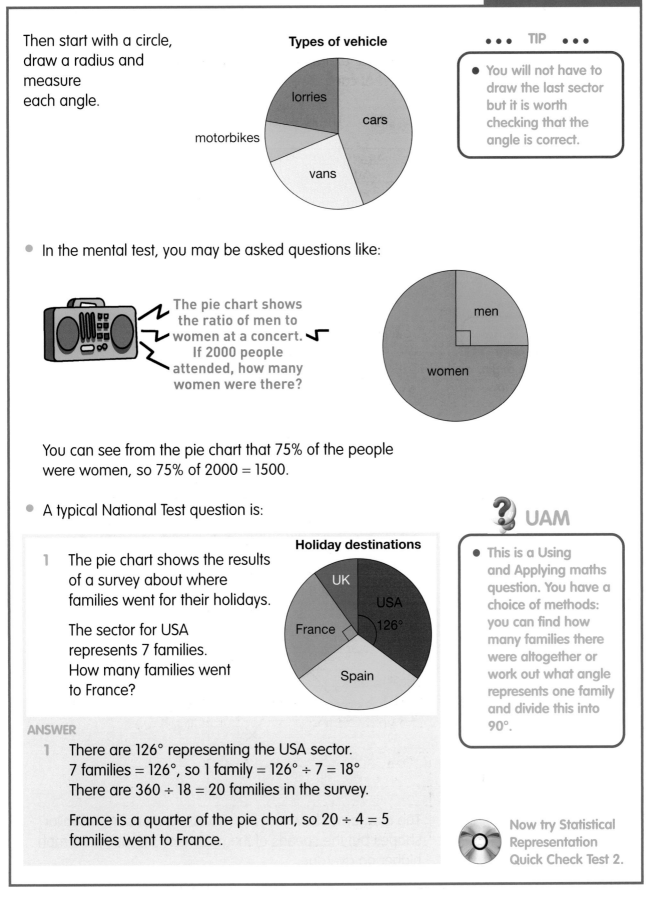

Then start with a circle, draw a radius and measure each angle.

Types of vehicle

lorries
cars
motorbikes
vans

● In the mental test, you may be asked questions like:

The pie chart shows the ratio of men to women at a concert. If 2000 people attended, how many women were there?

men
women

You can see from the pie chart that 75% of the people were women, so 75% of 2000 = 1500.

● A typical National Test question is:

? UAM

1   The pie chart shows the results of a survey about where families went for their holidays.

The sector for USA represents 7 families. How many families went to France?

Holiday destinations

UK
USA
France
126°
Spain

ANSWER

1   There are 126° representing the USA sector.
7 families = 126°, so 1 family = 126° ÷ 7 = 18°
There are 360 ÷ 18 = 20 families in the survey.

France is a quarter of the pie chart, so 20 ÷ 4 = 5 families went to France.

Now try Statistical Representation Quick Check Test 2.

KEY ! WORDS

- frequency diagram
- continuous data

- Continuous data is data that can take any value within a range, for example: height of plants, weight of cattle and speed of cars.

Example   The table shows the speeds of 100 cars on the M1.

Speed, s (mph)	Frequency
$50 < s \leq 60$	20
$60 < s \leq 70$	34
$70 < s \leq 80$	30
$80 < s \leq 90$	16

The diagram shows the speeds of 100 cars on the B1026.

••• TIP •••

- You do not have to join the first point plotted to the origin. The lines just show the shape of the distribution.

••• TIPS •••

- If you are asked to compare distributions, comment on the shape, the spread, (if it is significantly different) and the average values.
- The average will be in about the middle of the distribution.

On the same grid, draw a frequency diagram to show the speeds of the cars on the M1.

Comment on the differences between the two diagrams.

To draw the frequency diagram, plot the middle points of the groups against the frequencies and join up the points.

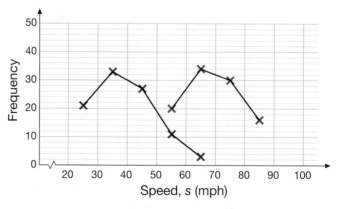

The diagrams show that the two distributions have similar shapes but the speeds of the motorway are about 30 mph higher on average.

● Typical National Test questions are:

1 The graph shows the time taken by a group of boys to run 100 metres.

The table shows the time taken by a group of girls to run 100 metres.

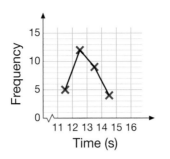

Time, t (seconds)	Frequency
$12 < t \leq 13$	7
$13 < t \leq 14$	8
$14 < t \leq 15$	8
$15 < t \leq 16$	7

Draw a frequency diagram on the same graph to represent the girls' times. Comment on the differences.

●●● TIP ●●●

● Plot the midpoint of the bar against the frequency.

There is a clue on how to do this on the diagram already drawn.

ANSWER

1 The girls' distribution is more even and their average time is higher.

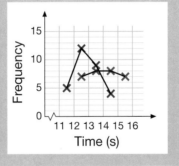

2 The dual bar chart shows the Test results for 40 boys and 40 girls.
A teacher says, 'The girls did better in the test than the boys'. Is she right? Explain your answer.

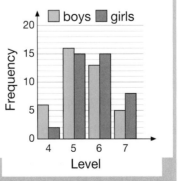

●●● TIP ●●●

● A dual bar chart has two sets of bars for different groups. There will also be a key showing which groups are represented by the different bars.

ANSWER

2 There is not much difference between the boys and girls but the girls have achieved more levels 6 and 7, so they did a little better than the boys.

Now try Statistical Representation Quick Check Test 3.

SCATTER DIAGRAMS

KEY **!** WORDS

- scatter diagrams
- variable
- correlation
- line of best fit

- A **scatter diagram** shows the relationship between two variables, for example: the temperature and the sales of ice-cream.

- The mathematical name for the relationship is **correlation**.

  The following diagrams show the different types of correlation.

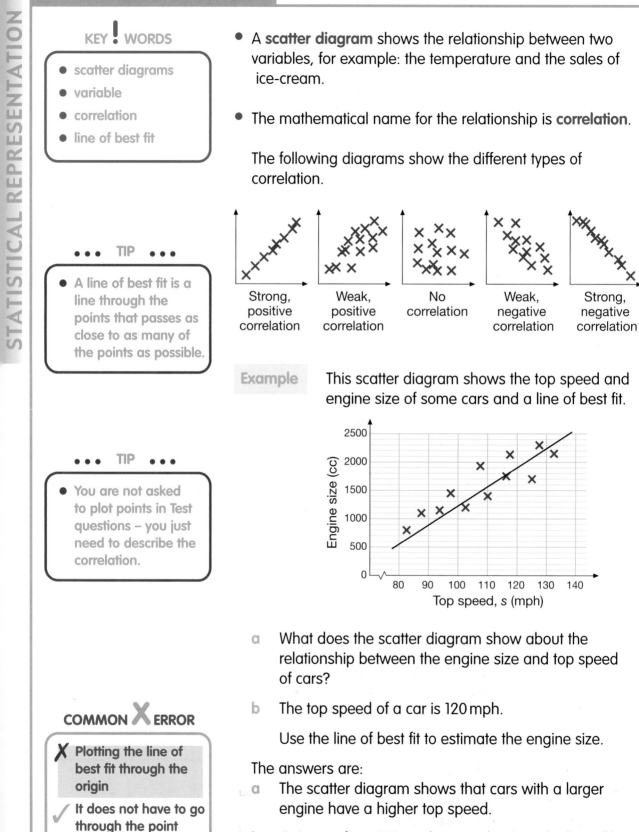

| Strong, positive correlation | Weak, positive correlation | No correlation | Weak, negative correlation | Strong, negative correlation |

••• TIP •••

- A line of best fit is a line through the points that passes as close to as many of the points as possible.

••• TIP •••

- You are not asked to plot points in Test questions – you just need to describe the correlation.

Example This scatter diagram shows the top speed and engine size of some cars and a line of best fit.

a What does the scatter diagram show about the relationship between the engine size and top speed of cars?

b The top speed of a car is 120 mph.

Use the line of best fit to estimate the engine size.

The answers are:

a The scatter diagram shows that cars with a larger engine have a higher top speed.

b Going up from 120 on the speed axis to the line of best fit and across to the engine size axis gives 1900 cc.

COMMON ✗ ERROR

✗ Plotting the line of best fit through the origin

✓ It does not have to go through the point where the axes meet.

- A typical National Test question is:

1 A fish breeder keeps records of the age and weight of his prize carp. He plots the results on a scatter diagram.

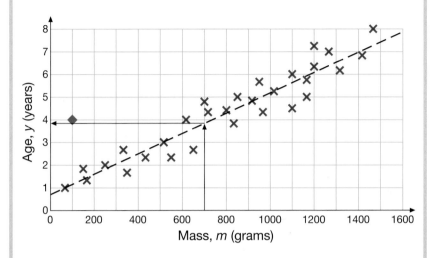

a A fish is 4 years old and weighs 100 g.
Explain why this fish is not likely to be a carp.

b The breeder is given a carp that weighs 700 g but he does not know how old it is.

He only uses fish for breeding if they are over 5 years old. Will this fish be suitable for breeding?
Give a reason for your answer.

• • • TIP • • •

- When using a line of best fit to find a value, it is a good idea to draw lines on the graph to show where your answer came from. This is especially true if you draw your own line of best fit.

 UAM

- This is a Using and Applying maths question. You have to decide on the strategy to find the age of the fish and then reach a conclusion.

ANSWERS

1 a The data shows strong positive correlation.
Plot the point (100, 4). (This is shown as a diamond.)

It is clear that this point is well away from the others, so it is unlikely to be a carp as it does not have the same correlation as the other values.

b Draw the line of best fit. (This is shown dashed.)

Draw lines from 700 g up to the line of best fit and then across to the age axis. (These are the solid lines.)

This comes to just under 4 years.
Hence the fish may not be old enough for breeding.

 Now try Statistical Representation Quick Check Test 4.

SURVEYS

KEY ! WORDS

- survey
- bias
- questionnaire
- response
- sample
- biased sample
- representative sample

- **Surveys** are used to find out information. Groups, such as the government, need information so they can plan for the future. Companies need to know who buys their products.

- Information is usually collected using a **questionnaire**.

  For example, if you want to find out if pupils would like to have a disco, you would want to know what day they would prefer, what type of refreshments, what type of music and how much they would pay.

- Questions in a questionnaire should be **unbiased**.

  This question is biased as it forces an opinion on the person being surveyed:

  > You would prefer a disco on Friday, wouldn't you?
  >
  > Yes ☐   No ☐

  A better question would be:

  > On which day would you prefer a disco?
  >
  > Thursday ☐   Friday ☐   Saturday ☐

- Questions should also have a simple response section, especially if you are collecting numerical answers.

  The response section of this question has overlapping boxes:

  > How old are you?
  > Under 10 ☐   10–20 ☐   20–30 ☐   Over 30 ☐

  A better question would be:

  > How old are you?
  > Under 10 ☐   11–20 ☐   21–30 ☐   31 or over ☐

••• TIPS •••

- Keep questions short and with a small choice of answers.
- Make your responses simple so you can use tick boxes.

••• TIP •••

- Don't ask personal questions such as 'How old are you' and expect an answer. People may be embarrassed to give their age.

  Give a range of possible answers.

- You also need to be very careful about where you take a survey and who you ask.

  If the school has a Friday lunchtime disco and you did your survey there, you would get a **biased sample** as the pupils are likely to say 'yes' to wanting a disco.

  If you just asked a Year 7 tutor group, then they may not want a disco and the views of the Year 11s would not be taken into account. This would be a **non-representative sample**.

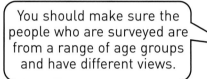

You should make sure the people who are surveyed are from a range of age groups and have different views.

- A typical National Test question is:

---

1 Year 7 are planning a trip and some pupils decide to do a survey about where people want to go.

   a This is one of Ricky's questions.

   > Do you want to go to Alton Towers ?
   > ☐ Yes   ☐ No

   What is wrong with this question?

   b This is another question.

   > How much are you willing to spend ?
   > £0–£5 ☐   £0–£10 ☐   Over £10 ☐

   What is wrong with this question?

   c Ricky decides to ask all the boys in his football practice group. What is wrong with this method of doing the survey?

ANSWERS

1 a There are not enough choices. Ricky is probably trying to get everyone to agree to go to Alton Towers.

   b The responses overlap so someone wanting to spend £4 would have two boxes to tick.

   c They will all have similar opinions. The sample is non-representative and will give a biased response.

Now try Statistical Representation Quick Check Test 5.

Also try Statistical Representation Final Test.

PROBABILITY 1

KEY ! WORDS

- probability
- chance
- event
- outcomes
- certain
- impossible
- at random
- mutually exclusive

- Probability is the chance that something will happen.
- An event that is impossible has a probability of 0.

  An event that is certain has a probability of 1.

  All other probabilities are between 0 and 1.

- The probability scale runs from 0 to 1.

- Various words can be used to describe probability such as: impossible, very unlikely, unlikely, evens, likely, very likely and certain.

  On a probability scale these would be:

Impossible	Very unlikely	Unlikely	Evens	Likely	Very likely	Certain

  0   1

Example   The probabilities of various events are shown on the scale below:

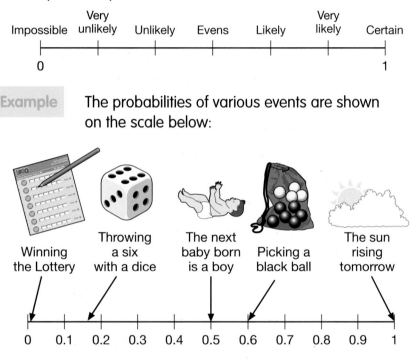

Winning the Lottery   Throwing a six with a dice   The next baby born is a boy   Picking a black ball   The sun rising tomorrow

0   0.1   0.2   0.3   0.4   0.5   0.6   0.7   0.8   0.9   1

If the chance of picking a black ball from the bag shown above is $\frac{6}{10}$ or $\frac{3}{5}$, what is the chance of picking a white ball?

You can see that there are four white balls so the chance of picking a white ball is $\frac{4}{10}$ or $\frac{2}{5}$.

Note that $\frac{6}{10} + \frac{4}{10} = 1$ and $\frac{3}{5} + \frac{2}{5} = 1$

> The total probability of all possible events is 1.
> These are known as mutually exclusive events:
> P(Boy) + P(Girl) = 1, P(Head) + P(Tail) = 1.

COMMON ✗ ERROR

✗ Writing probabilities in words or as a ratio.

For example, the chance of throwing a six with a dice is $\frac{1}{6}$. It should not be written as 1 in 6, 1 out of 6 or 1 : 6.

✓ Probabilities should always be written as fractions, decimals or percentages.

• • • TIP • • •

- 'The probability of' can be written as P(...) =, so the probability of a head when tossing a coin is P(Head) = $\frac{1}{2}$

- Typical National Test questions are:

1 A bag contains 7 blue balls and 1 red ball.

a Robyn is going to take a ball at random from the bag. She says, 'There are two colours so it is equally as likely that I will take a blue ball as a red ball'. Explain why Robyn is wrong.

b Complete the sentences using these words:

impossible very unlikely unlikely evens likely very likely certain

A ball is taken at random from the bag.
The probability of taking a blue ball is ....
The probability of taking a green ball is ....

c How many red balls must be put in the bag to make the chance of taking a red ball evens?

ANSWERS

1 a There are unequal numbers of each colour in the bag. The probability of blue is $\frac{7}{8}$ and red is $\frac{1}{8}$.

b The probability of getting a blue ball is very likely. The probability of getting a green ball is impossible.

c To make the probability evens there should be the same number of each colour. So 6 red balls need to be added.

2 A box of juice drinks contains four orange, three grapefruit, two cranberry and one lemon drink. A drink is taken at random from the box.

a What is the probability it is orange?

b What is the probability that it is not lemon?

c Mary drinks two orange juices. She then takes a drink at random from the remaining drinks. What is the probability she takes a cranberry juice?

ANSWERS

2 a P(orange) = $\frac{4}{10}$ = $\frac{2}{5}$ b P(not lemon) = $\frac{9}{10}$

c There are 8 drinks left; 2 are cranberry.
So P(cranberry) = $\frac{2}{8}$ = $\frac{1}{4}$

••• TIP •••

- You need to add up the total number of balls to find the denominator of the fraction.

••• TIP •••

- Unless the question asks for an answer in 'its simplest form', you do not have to cancel fractions, but be careful if you do.

••• TIP •••

- There are 9 out of 10 that are not lemon but it can also be worked out as:

1 – P(lemon)

$1 - \frac{1}{10} = \frac{9}{10}$

Now try Probability Quick Check Test 1.

PROBABILITY 2

- probability
- chance
- event
- certain
- impossible
- relative frequency

● The probability of an event is the number of ways that event can happen divided by the total number of outcomes. Consider throwing a two with a dice. There is one way of throwing a two and six ways the dice can land, so P(2 with a dice) = $\frac{1}{6}$.

Example   When a dice is thrown, what is the probability of:

a   a score of 4   b a square number   c a factor of 24?

The dice can land six ways.

a   There is only one 4 so P(4) = $\frac{1}{6}$

b   Square numbers are 1 and 4, so P(square) = $\frac{2}{6}$ = $\frac{1}{3}$

c   The factors of 24 on a dice are 1, 2, 3, 4, 6 so

   P(factors of 24) = $\frac{5}{6}$

● In the mental test you may be asked questions like:

There are 6 red and 3 blue balls in a bag. One ball is taken from the bag at random.
What is the probability that it will be blue?

... TIP ...

- You do not need to cancel fractions to receive full marks.

There are three blue balls out of nine altogether. The probability of a blue ball is $\frac{3}{9}$ = $\frac{1}{3}$.

● You could also be asked questions such as:

A box of toffee contains hard and soft toffees only. The probability of taking a hard toffee is $\frac{8}{15}$.
What is the probability of taking a soft toffee?

... TIP ...

- To subtract $\frac{8}{15}$ from 1, the denominator stays the same and the numerator is

  15 − 8 = 7

  1 − $\frac{8}{15}$ = $\frac{7}{15}$

The probability of a hard toffee is $\frac{8}{15}$, so the probability of a soft toffee is 1 − $\frac{8}{15}$ = $\frac{7}{15}$.

• Typical National Test questions are:

1   Mark has the following cards:

$\boxed{S}\boxed{T}\boxed{A}\boxed{T}\boxed{I}\boxed{S}\boxed{T}\boxed{I}\boxed{C}\boxed{S}$

He picks one at random.
a   The letter he picks has a probability of $\frac{1}{5}$ of being chosen. What letter did he pick?

b   What is the probability that he picks a letter S?

c   What is the probability that the letter he picks is not a vowel?

ANSWERS

1   a   There are 10 cards and $\frac{1}{5} = \frac{2}{10}$.
        The only letter that occurs twice is I.

    b   There are three Ss, so P(S) = $\frac{3}{10}$

    c   There are three vowels so P(vowel) = $\frac{3}{10}$.
        P(not a vowel) = $1 - \frac{3}{10} = \frac{7}{10}$.

2   A box contains 21 copper nails and 9 steel nails.
    A nail is taken out at random.
    a   What is the probability that it is a copper nail?
        Give your answer as a fraction in its simplest form.

    b   Give your answer to part a as a percentage.

    c   Six nails are taken out of the box.
        After the nails are removed, the probability of taking a copper nail at random is $\frac{7}{8}$.
        Explain how you know that the six nails taken out were steel nails.

ANSWERS

2   a   P(copper) = $\frac{21}{30} = \frac{7}{10}$

    b $\frac{7}{10}$ = 70%

    c   There are now 24 nails in the box.
        If P(copper) = $\frac{7}{8} = \frac{21}{24}$, then there are still 21 copper nails in the box. So the nails removed must have been steel nails.

••• TIP •••

• There are 7 letters that are vowels so P(not vowel) = $\frac{7}{10}$.

••• TIP •••

• You need to know the equivalent decimals and percentages for some simple fractions.

? UAM

• This is a Using and Applying maths question – you have to use reasoning to answer part (c).

Now try Probability Quick Check Test 2.

KEY ! WORDS

- independent events
- two way tables
- combined events
- sample space

••• TIP •••

- You will usually be told which way to write out all the outcomes.

- Sometimes two separate events can take place at the same time, for example throwing a dice and tossing a coin.

- The mathematical name for events like this is independent, because the outcome of throwing the dice does not have any influence on the outcome of tossing the coin.

- The combined outcomes of the two events can be shown in different ways.

- They can be written as a list:

(1, head), (1, tail), (2, head), (2, tail), (3, head), (3, tail), (4, head), (4, tail), (5, head), (5, tail), (6, head), (6, tail)

- They can also be shown in a sample space diagram:

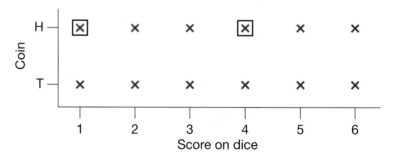

- You can see that there are 12 outcomes for the combined events.

So to work out the probability of throwing a head with the coin and a square number on the dice you would need to count which of the 12 outcomes satisfy the conditions.

These are shown in a box on the sample space diagram.

So P(head and square number) $= \frac{2}{12} = \frac{1}{6}$

● A typical National Test question is:

1 Two four-sided dice numbered from 1 to 4 are thrown together. The scores are multiplied together.

a Complete the sample space diagram showing the possible scores of the combined event.

Score on second dice

	1	2	3	4
1	1	2		
2			6	
3		6	9	
4	4	8	12	16

Score on first dice

b Find the probability that the combined score is:
i an even number
ii a square number
iii a factor of 144

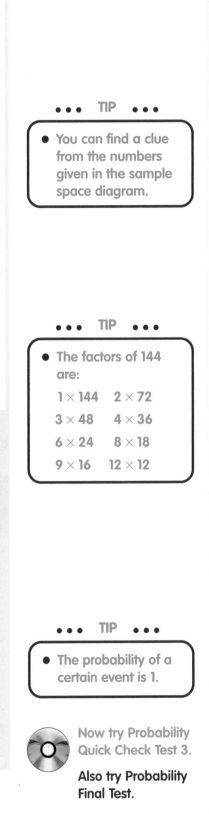

••• TIP •••

● You can find a clue from the numbers given in the sample space diagram.

••• TIP •••

● The factors of 144 are:

1×144 2×72
3×48 4×36
6×24 8×18
9×16 12×12

ANSWERS

1 a

Score on second dice

	1	2	3	4
1	1	2	3	4
2	2	4	6	8
3	3	6	9	12
4	4	8	12	16

Score on first dice

b i There are 16 outcomes and 12 of them are even numbers. P(even) = $\frac{12}{16}$ = $\frac{3}{4}$
ii There are 6 square numbers: 1, 4, 4, 4, 9, 16
P(square) = $\frac{6}{16}$ = $\frac{3}{8}$
iii All of the numbers are factors of 144.
P(factor of 144) = 1

••• TIP •••

● The probability of a certain event is 1.

Now try Probability Quick Check Test 3.

Also try Probability Final Test.

Time allowed 40 minutes
You may not use a calculator on this paper.

1   The diagram shows a rectangle.
    Its length is 4.2 cm and its width is 2.5 cm.

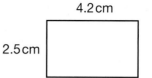

4.2 cm

2.5 cm

   a Two of the rectangles are joined together in different ways to make
   two new rectangles.

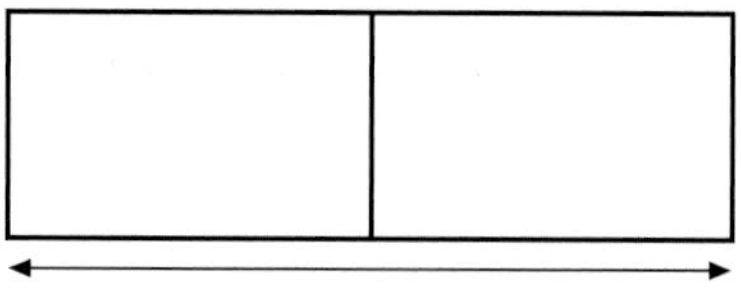

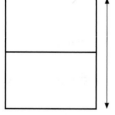

   9   11.5

   ||| | |

   The length of this rectangle is _____ cm.   *1 mark*

   The width of this rectangle is _____ cm.   *1 mark*

   b How many of the rectangles are needed to make a new rectangle with a
   width of 15 cm?

   _____   *1 mark*

2   Reflect each shape
    in the given
    mirror line.

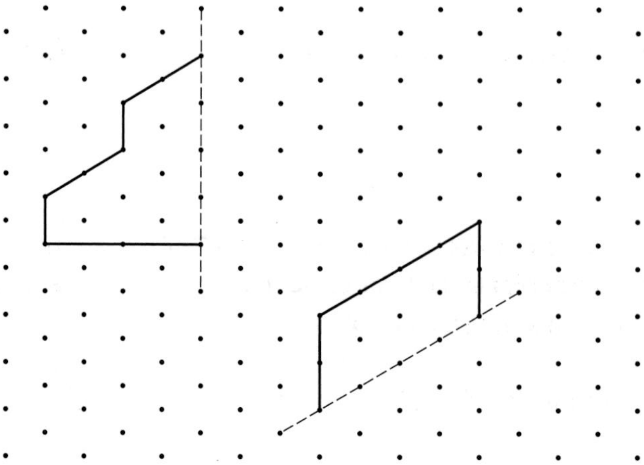

                                                              2 marks

3 Brian buys a computer costing £1040.
He pays a deposit of £200.
He then pays the remainder in six equal instalments.
How much is each instalment?

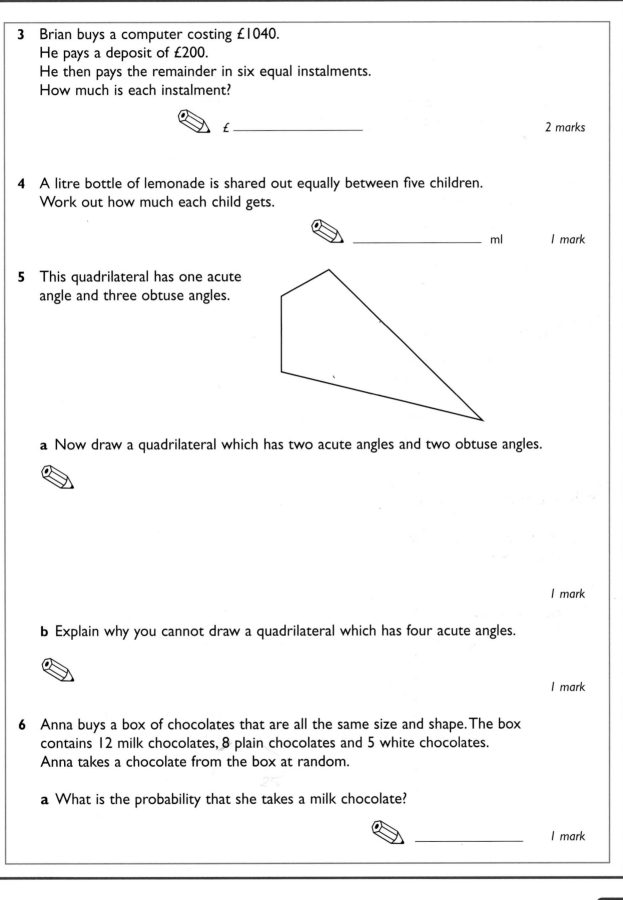 £ _____

2 marks

4 A litre bottle of lemonade is shared out equally between five children.
Work out how much each child gets.

_____ ml   1 mark

5 This quadrilateral has one acute
angle and three obtuse angles.

a Now draw a quadrilateral which has two acute angles and two obtuse angles.

1 mark

b Explain why you cannot draw a quadrilateral which has four acute angles.

1 mark

6 Anna buys a box of chocolates that are all the same size and shape. The box
contains 12 milk chocolates, 8 plain chocolates and 5 white chocolates.
Anna takes a chocolate from the box at random.

a What is the probability that she takes a milk chocolate?

_____   1 mark

b What is the probability that she takes a plain chocolate?

_____ *1 mark*

c What is the probability that she does not take a white chocolate?

_____ *1 mark*

7 A single ticket on the metro costs £1.35.
Dave buys a book of 25 single tickets, which costs him £30.
How much does Dave save by buying a book of tickets?

£ _____ *2 marks*

8 When $a = 6$, $b = 5$ and $c = 2$,
a work out the value of the following:

$a + 2b + c$ _____ *1 mark*

$3a + b - 2c$ _____ *1 mark*

b If $a + b + c + d = 20$, work out the value of d. _____ *1 mark*

9 Here is a fraction strip.

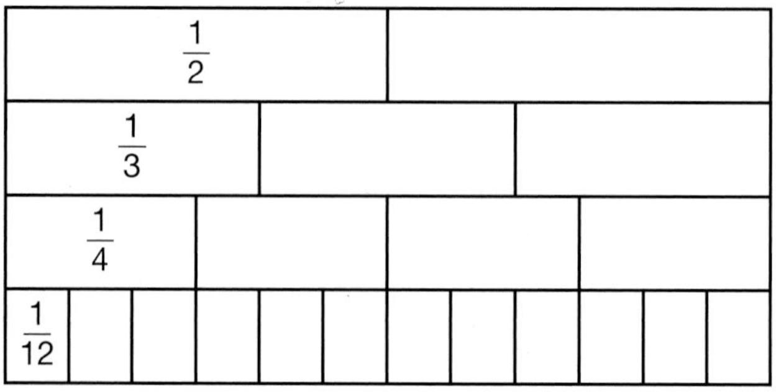

$\frac{1}{2}$	
$\frac{1}{3}$		
$\frac{1}{4}$			
$\frac{1}{12}$											

Use the fraction strip to help you work out the following:

$\frac{1}{2} + \frac{5}{12} =$ *1 mark*

$\frac{1}{4} + \frac{1}{3} =$ *1 mark*

$\frac{3}{4} - \frac{5}{12} =$ *1 mark*

10 a Complete the table for the mapping $y = x + 5$.

x	2	4	6
y	7		

1 mark

b Complete the table for the mapping $y = 2x^2 - 3$.

x	2	4	6
y	1		

1 mark

c Write down the mapping for this table.

x	2	4	6
y	2	3	4

$y =$ _____ *1 mark*

11 Here are three cuboids.

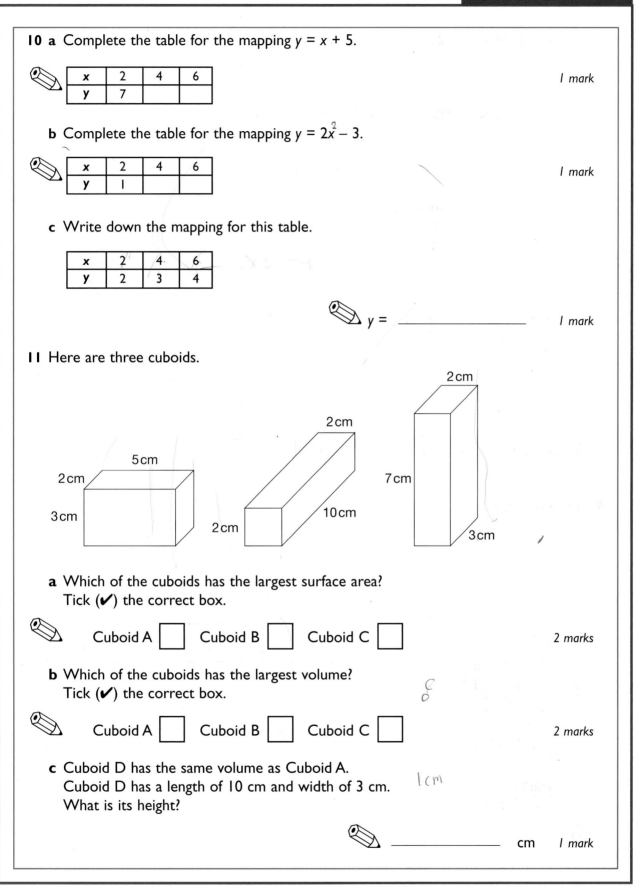

a Which of the cuboids has the largest surface area?
Tick (✔) the correct box.

Cuboid A ☐   Cuboid B ☐   Cuboid C ☐

2 marks

b Which of the cuboids has the largest volume?
Tick (✔) the correct box.

Cuboid A ☐   Cuboid B ☐   Cuboid C ☐

2 marks

c Cuboid D has the same volume as Cuboid A.
Cuboid D has a length of 10 cm and width of 3 cm.
What is its height?

_____ cm   *1 mark*

12 Three quadrilaterals are drawn on square grids below.

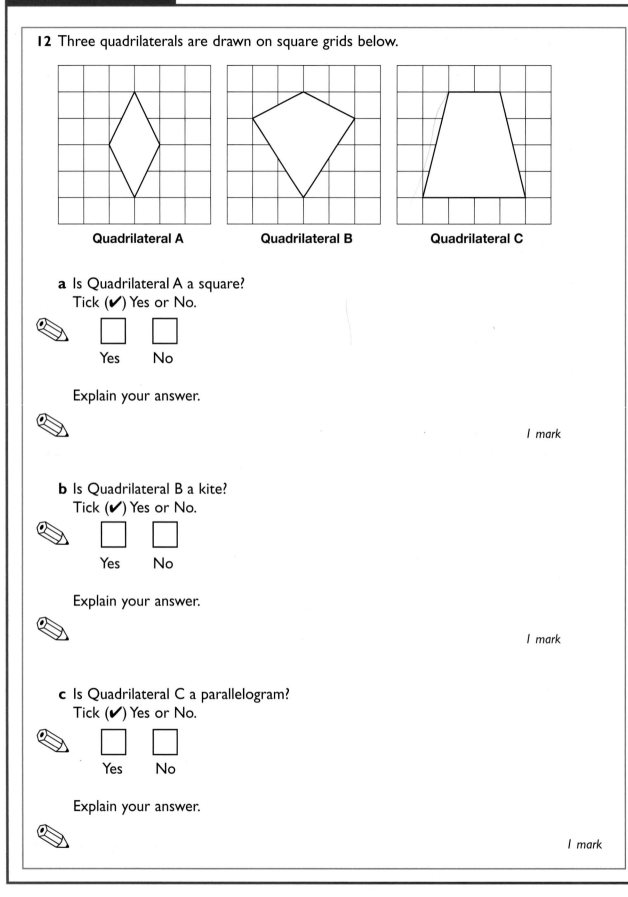

Quadrilateral A   **Quadrilateral B**   **Quadrilateral C**

a Is Quadrilateral A a square?
Tick (✔) Yes or No.

☐ Yes   ☐ No

Explain your answer.

1 mark

b Is Quadrilateral B a kite?
Tick (✔) Yes or No.

☐ Yes   ☐ No

Explain your answer.

1 mark

c Is Quadrilateral C a parallelogram?
Tick (✔) Yes or No.

☐ Yes   ☐ No

Explain your answer.

1 mark

13 Fill in the missing numbers in the boxes.

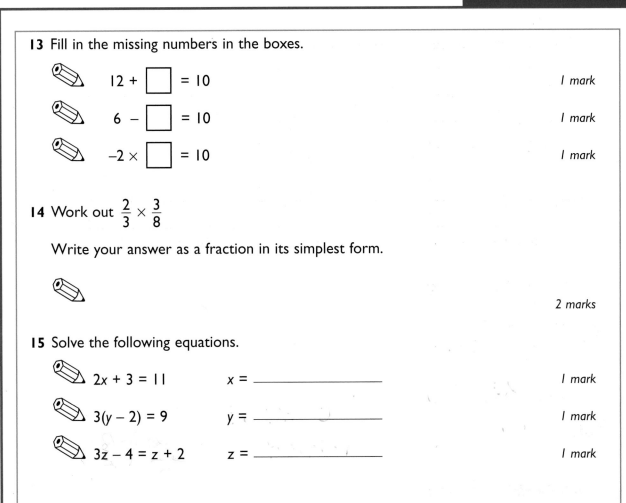

$12 + \boxed{} = 10$ *1 mark*

$6 - \boxed{} = 10$ *1 mark*

$-2 \times \boxed{} = 10$ *1 mark*

14 Work out $\dfrac{2}{3} \times \dfrac{3}{8}$

Write your answer as a fraction in its simplest form.

2 marks

15 Solve the following equations.

$2x + 3 = 11$ $x = $ _____   *1 mark*

$3(y - 2) = 9$ $y = $ _____   *1 mark*

$3z - 4 = z + 2$ $z = $ _____   *1 mark*

Answers are on page 137.

TEST PAPER 2

Time allowed 40 minutes
You may use a calculator on this paper.

1 Here is a shaded shape on a 1 cm grid.

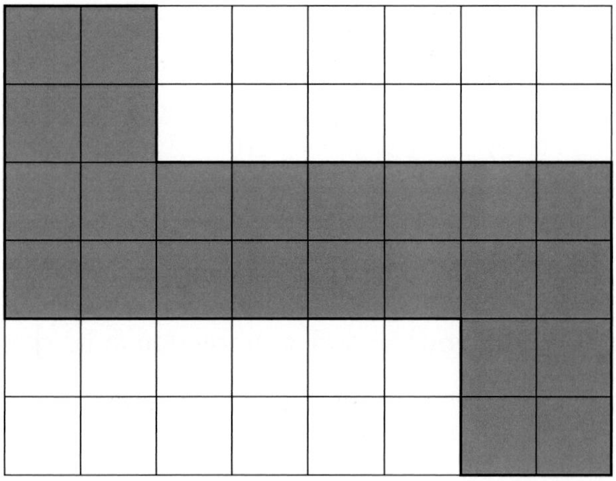

a What is the area of the shape?

_______________ cm^2

1 mark

b The shape is the net of a cube.
What is the volume of the cube?

____

2 marks

c Now draw a rectangle that has the same area as the shaded shape.

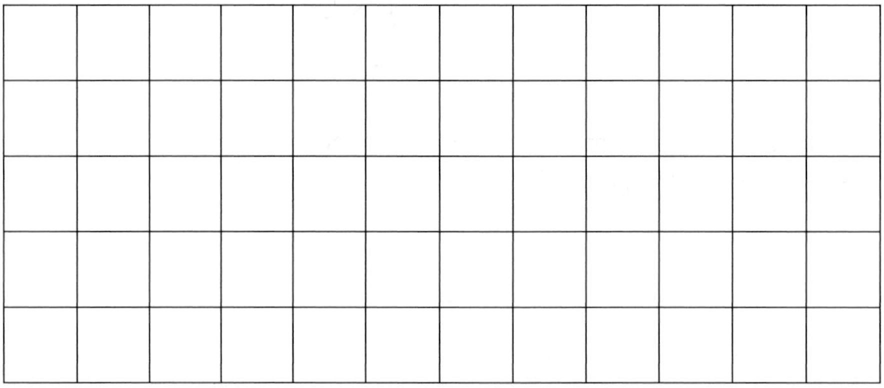

1 mark

2 **a** VAT in Britain is charged at $17\frac{1}{2}$%.
A camera is priced as £280 excluding VAT.
What is $17\frac{1}{2}$% of £280?

£ _______________

2 marks

b In America, sales tax is charged on goods.
A camera costing $120 excluding sales tax had $6.00 sales tax added
to the price.
What percentage of 120 is 6?

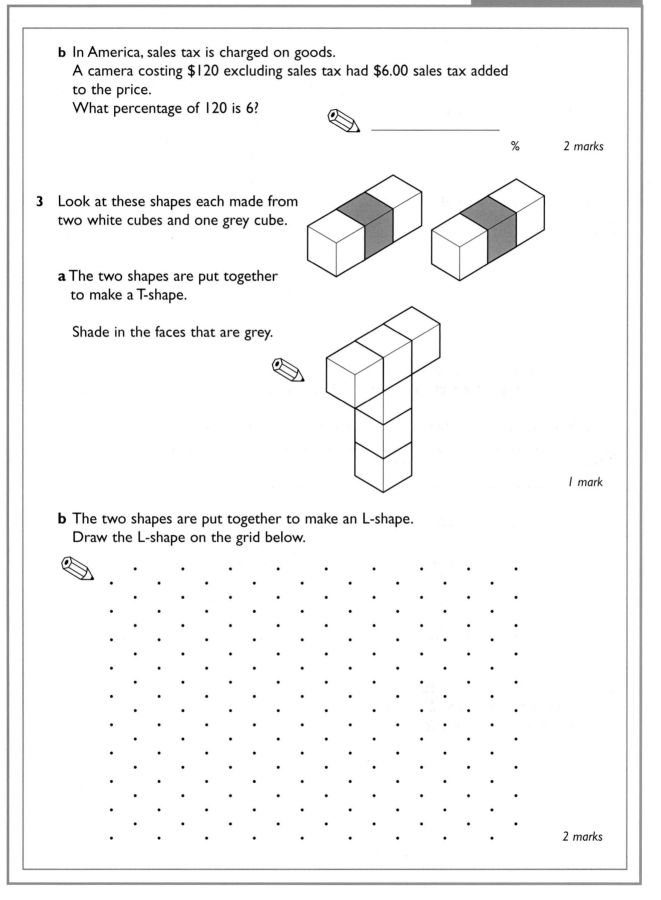

_____

%   *2 marks*

3 Look at these shapes each made from
two white cubes and one grey cube.

a The two shapes are put together
to make a T-shape.

Shade in the faces that are grey.

1 mark

b The two shapes are put together to make an L-shape.
Draw the L-shape on the grid below.

2 marks

4 The pie chart shows the replies to a survey on holiday destinations.

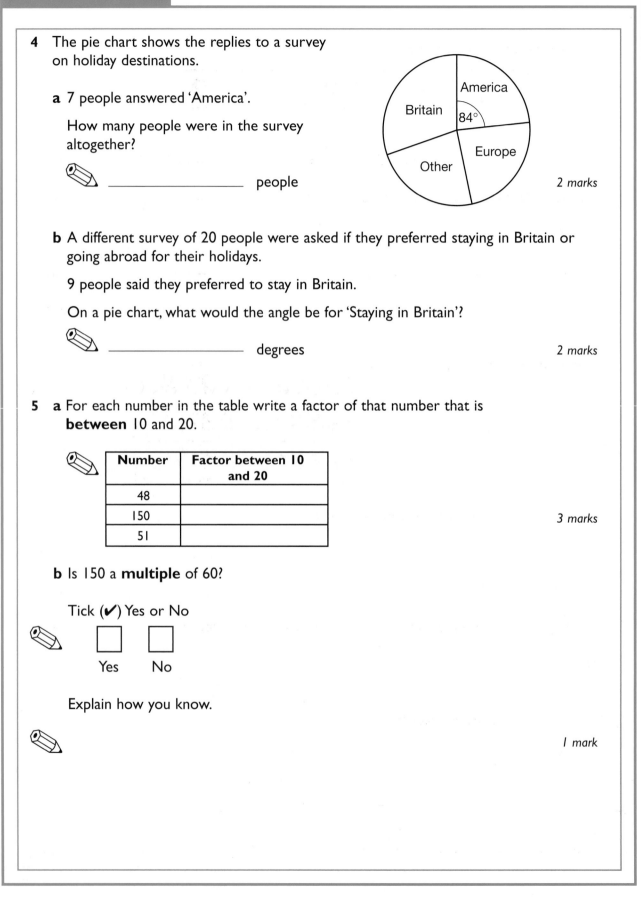

a 7 people answered 'America'.

How many people were in the survey altogether?

_____ people

2 marks

b A different survey of 20 people were asked if they preferred staying in Britain or going abroad for their holidays.

9 people said they preferred to stay in Britain.

On a pie chart, what would the angle be for 'Staying in Britain'?

_____ degrees

2 marks

5 a For each number in the table write a factor of that number that is **between** 10 and 20.

Number	Factor between 10 and 20
48	
150	
51	

3 marks

b Is 150 a **multiple** of 60?

Tick (✔) Yes or No

☐ ☐
Yes No

Explain how you know.

1 mark

6 Here are eight number cards.

$$\boxed{-3}\ \boxed{-1}\ \boxed{-1}\ \boxed{0}\ \boxed{2}\ \boxed{6}\ \boxed{8}\ \boxed{9}$$

a What is the range of the numbers? _____ *1 mark*

b What is the sum of the numbers? _____ *1 mark*

c What is the mode of the numbers? _____ *1 mark*

d What is the median of the numbers? _____ *1 mark*

e What is the mean of the numbers? _____ *2 marks*

7 Here is part of a number grid.

23	24	25	26	27	28
33	34	35	36	37	38
43	44	45	46	47	48

From these numbers, write down one that is:

a a prime number _____ *1 mark*

b a square number _____ *1 mark*

c Explain why a square number could never be a prime number. *1 mark*

_____

8 a ABC is an isosceles triangle.

What is angle *p*?

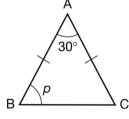

_____ degrees *1 mark*

b This diagram is not drawn accurately.

Calculate the size of angle m.

Show your working.

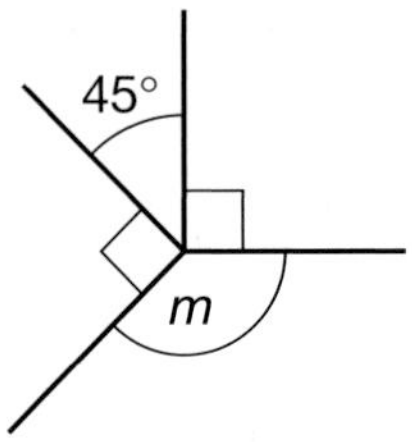

✏ _____ degrees

1 mark

45°

m

9 A 50p coin has a mass of 8 grams.

How much is one kilogram of 50p coins worth?

✏ £ _____

3 marks

10 The graph shows a straight line.

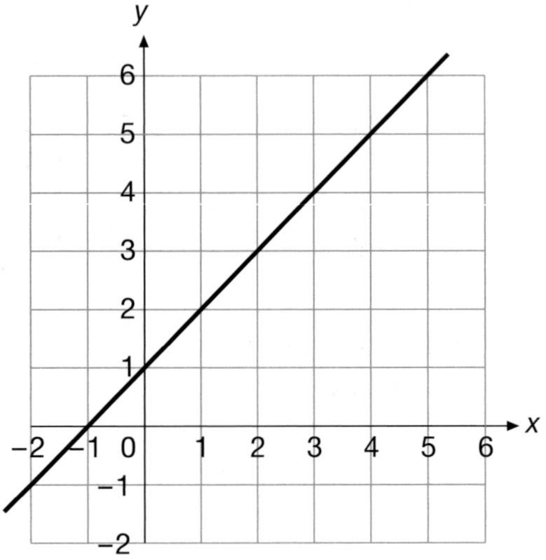

a Fill in the table with some of the points on the line.

✏

(x, y)	(…, …)	(…, …)	(…, …)
x + 1			

b Write down the equation of the line.

✏ _____

2 marks

1 mark

c On the graph draw the line $y = x + 3$

1 mark

11 A bicycle wheel has a diameter of 70 cm.

a What is the circumference of the wheel?

✏ _____ cm

1 mark

b During a 5 kilometre race, approximately how many times will the wheel turn?

✏ _____ turns

70 cm

2 marks

Answers are on page 139.

In your mental mathematics test, you will hear the questions and write your answers on the answer sheets. For the first group of questions you will have 5 seconds to work out each answer and write it down.

Time: 5 seconds

1   Multiply forty-three by ten.

| 1 | | |

2   How many metres are in 300 centimetres?

| 2 | | 300 cm | |

3   What is one-fifth of thirty-five?

| 3 | | |

4   Subtract four from minus six.

| 4 | | −6 | |

5   Look at the equation. When x equals six, what is the value of y?

| 5 | | $y = x^2 - 5$ | |

6   What is four point five divided by two?

| 6 | | 4.5 | |

7   To the nearest ten kilometres the length of a motorway is ninety kilometres.

What is the least value the length of the motorway could be?

| 7 | km | |

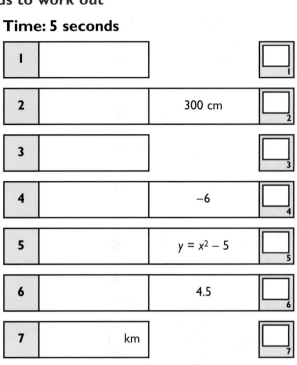

For the next group of questions you will have 10 seconds to work out each answer and write it down.

Time: 10 seconds

8   The chart shows the number of hours of TV watched by a child in a week.

On which day was 3 hours of TV watched?

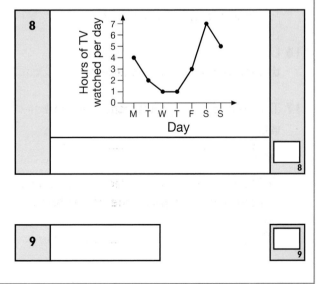

9   A robot moves so that it is always the same distance from a fixed point.

What is the name of the shape of the robot's path?

| 9 | | |

10 Look at the grid. Write down the coordinates of the point B.

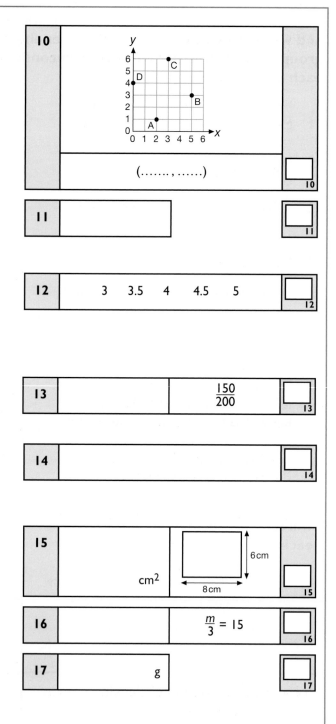

10	

(......., ...)

| | 10 |

11 How many fifths are there in two?

11	
	11

12 Think about the mass two kilograms.

About how many pounds is that?

Circle the best answer on the answer sheet.

12	3 3.5 4 4.5 5
	12

13 Look at the fraction.

Write it in its simplest form.

13		$\frac{150}{200}$
		13

14 In a survey one-third of the people asked preferred to go abroad for their holidays.

What percentage is this?

14	
	14

15 What is the area of this rectangle?

15		
	cm²	6cm / 8cm
		15

16 Look at the equation. Solve it to find the value of *m*.

16		$\frac{m}{3} = 15$
		16

17 The average weight of a male squirrel is 500 grams.

Female squirrels have an average weight that is 5% less than this.

What is the average weight of a female squirrel?

17	g
	17

18 A cardboard box measures half a metre by thirty centimetres by twenty centimetres.

Which of the calculations on the answer sheet will give the volume of the box?

Ring the correct answer.

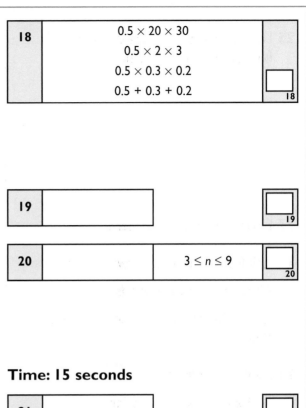

18	
	$0.5 \times 20 \times 30$
	$0.5 \times 2 \times 3$
	$0.5 \times 0.3 \times 0.2$
	$0.5 + 0.3 + 0.2$

19 What is a quarter of two thirds of sixty?

19		19

20 Look at the inequality.

How many integer solutions are there?

20		$3 \le n \le 9$	20

For the next group of questions you will have 15 seconds to work out each answer and write it down.

Time: 15 seconds

21 Write down a factor of 48 that is bigger than ten but less than twenty.

21		21

22 The first odd number is one. What is the hundredth odd number?

22		22

23 On the grid sketch the line $x + y = 4$.

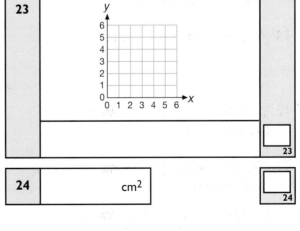

23		23

24 What is the area of circle with a radius of 3 centimetres?

Give your answer in terms of π.

24	cm^2	24

25 I can make twenty-four different four-digit numbers from the digits one, two, three and four.

How many of these will be odd numbers?

25	**1** **2** **3** **4**	
		25

26 Look at the calculation.

Write down an approximate answer.

26		$\dfrac{38.5 \times 51.6}{4.89}$	
			26

27 Complete the factorisation.

27	$x^2 - 16 = (x + 4)(\ldots\ldots\ldots)$	
		27

28 A bag contains only red and blue balls.

There are twice as many blue balls as red balls.

I take a ball at random from a bag.

What is the probability that the ball will be red?

28		
		28

29 What 3-D shape has four edges?

29		
		29

30 What is the sum of all the integers from 1 to 10?

30	1 2 3 4 5	
	6 7 8 9 10	
		30

Answers are on page 141.

Q	Mark	Correct response	Comments
1 a	1	8.4(cm)	Work out 4.2 + 4.2 or 4.2 × 2
	1	5 (cm) or 5.0 (cm)	Work out 2.5 + 2.5 or 2.5 × 2
b	1	6	Find the number of times 2.5 goes into 15, so work out 15 ÷ 2.5
2	1		You can check your answers with a mirror or tracing paper.
	1		For diagonal mirror lines, it is easier to turn the page round until the mirror line is horizontal.
3	2 or 1	(£)140

Showing a correct method, e.g. (1040 − 200) ÷ 6 | First work out 1040 − 200 = 840 to find the remainder, then each instalment is 840 ÷ 6 = 140 |
4	1	200 (ml)	1 litre = 1000 millilitres and 1000 ÷ 5 = 200
5 a	1	For example,	Acute angles are less than 90° and obtuse angles are between 90° and 180°.
b	1	An acute angle is less than 90° and four times a number less than 90 must be less than 360.	This is a Using and Applying maths question. In your answer, you must show that you know the sum of the angles in a quadrilateral is 360°.
6 a	1	$\frac{12}{25}$	Your answers to this question must be written as a fraction. Answers such as 12 out of 25 or 12 in 25 or 12 : 25 are not acceptable.
b	1	$\frac{8}{25}$	
c	1	$\frac{20}{25}$ or $\frac{4}{5}$	20 chocolates are not white. You would not lose the mark if you did not cancel down the fraction.
7	2 or 1	(£)3.75

digits 3375 seen | Use a suitable method to work out 1.35 × 25, which is 33.75. The saving is 33.75 − 30 = 3.75 |

				Work out $6 + (2 \times 5) + 2 = 6 + 10 + 2$
8 a	I	18		Work out $6 + (2 \times 5) + 2 = 6 + 10 + 2$
	I	19		Work out $(3 \times 6) + 5 - (2 \times 2) = 18 + 5 - 4 = 19$
b	I	7		$a + b + c = 13$, so $d = 20 - 13 = 7$
9	I	$\frac{11}{12}$		$\frac{1}{2} = \frac{6}{12}$
	I	$\frac{7}{12}$		$\frac{1}{4} = \frac{3}{12}$ and $\frac{1}{3} = \frac{4}{12}$
	I	$\frac{4}{12}$ or $\frac{1}{3}$		$\frac{3}{4} = \frac{9}{12}$
10 a	I	x 2 4 6 y 7 9 11		The mapping $y = x + 5$ means add 5 to each x-value to get the y-value.
b	I	x 2 4 6 y 1 5 9		The mapping $y = 2x - 3$ means multiply each x-value by 2 and then subtract 3 to get the y-value.
c	I	$(y) = \frac{1}{2}x + 1$ or $(y) = x \div 2 + 1$		To get the y-value, you halve each x-value and then add 1.
11 a	2 or 1	Cuboid B		The surface area of a cuboid is the total area of its 6 faces. $A = 62 \text{ cm}^2$, $B = 88 \text{ cm}^2$, $C = 82 \text{ cm}^2$. You would get I mark for finding the correct surface area for two cuboids.
b	2 or 1	Cuboid C		The volume of a cuboid is $V = lwh$. $A = 30 \text{ cm}^3$, $B = 40 \text{ cm}^3$, $C = 42 \text{ cm}^3$. You would get I mark for finding the correct volume for two cuboids.
c	I	1 (cm)		$V = 10 \times 3 \times h$, so $30 = 30h$ and $h = 1$
12 a	I	No		The sides are the same length, but the 4 angles are not 90°, or it is a rhombus.
b	I	Yes		Two pairs of adjacent sides have the same length.
c	I	No		It only has one pair of parallel sides, or it is a trapezium.
13	I	-2		$12 + (-2) = 10$, since $+(-)$ is the same as $-$
	I	-4		$6 - (-4) = 10$, since $-(-)$ is the same as $+$
	I	-5		$-2 \times (-5) = 10$, since $- \times - = +$
14	2 or 1	$\frac{1}{4}$ $\frac{6}{24}$ or $\frac{3}{12}$		To multiply fractions, multiply the numerators and the denominators. You would get I mark for not cancelling.
15	I	$(x) = 4$		$2x = 8$ (take 3 from both sides) $x = 4$ (divide both sides by 2)
	I	$(y) = 5$		$3y - 6 = 9$ (multiply out brackets) $3y = 15$ (add 6 to both sides) $y = 5$ (divide both side by 3)
	I	$(z) = 3$		$2z - 4 = 2$ (take z from both sides) $2z = 6$ (add 4 to both sides) $z = 3$ (divide both sides by 2)

	Mark	Correct response	Comments
1 a	1	24 (cm²)	You can count squares or work out the areas of different squares and rectangles.
b	1	8	The cube is 2 cm by 2 cm by 2 cm.
	1	cm³	You need to show units if they are not given.
c	1	Any rectangle with correct area	Examples are 2 cm × 12 cm, 3 cm × 8 cm, 4 cm × 6 cm.
2 a	2 or 1	(£)49 Shows a correct method, e.g 17.5 ÷ 100 × 280	There are many ways of working this out. $17\frac{1}{2}$% of 280 means 17.5 hundredths of 280. This can be calculated by 0.175 × 280 or $\frac{175}{100}$ × 280
b	2 or 1	5(%) Shows a correct method, e.g 6 ÷ 120 × 100	The fraction is $\frac{6}{120}$ which cancels to $\frac{1}{20}$. You should know that $\frac{1}{20}$ is equivalent to 5%, or you can do the calculation 6 ÷ 120 × 100
3 a	1		All faces of the grey cube must be shaded.
b	2	For example,	Any L-shape in any orientation will gain full marks.
	or		
	1	For example,	Any L-shape using 5 cubes in any orientation will gain one mark.
4 a	2 or 1	30(people) 12 seen	84° is equivalent to 7 people, so 84 ÷ 7 = 12° is equivalent to 1 person. 360 ÷ 12 = 30
b	2 or 1	162(degrees) 18 seen	20 people in a pie chart will get 360 ÷ 20 = 18° per person. 9 people will be an angle of 9 × 18 = 162°

5 a	1	12 or 16	The factors of 48 are: {1, 2, 3, 4, 6, 8, 12, 16, 24, 48}. You can give both answers.
	1	15	The factors of 150 are: {1, 2, 3, 5, 10, 15, 30, 50, 75, 150}. 'Between' means that you do not include 10 or 20.
	1	17	The factors of 51 are: {1, 3, 17, 51}.
b	1	'No' ticked and an explanation such as '150 is not in the 60 times table'.	You need to make it clear that you understand that a multiple is in the times table so writing down 60, 120, 180, … would just about do this.
6 a	1	12	The range is the difference between the highest and the lowest numbers. From −3 to 9 is a difference of 12.
b	1	20	The total of the negative numbers is −5. The total of the positive numbers is 25. 25 − 5 = 20.
c	1	−1	The mode is the most common number.
d	1	1	The median is the middle number when the numbers are in order. These are already in order but there is an even number of values, so the median is between 0 and 2.
e	2 or 1	2.5 Showing a correct method, e.g. the total ÷ 8	The mean is the total of the numbers divided by how many numbers there are. The total is 20 and there are 8 values.
7 a	1	23 or 37 or 43 or 47	Prime numbers have no factors other than 1 and themselves. Only one answer is needed but you will not lose the mark if you give more than one.
b	1	25 or 36	Square numbers are numbers that can be written as 5 × 5 or 6 × 6, etc.
c	1	Because square numbers always have a factor other than 1 or itself.	You need to make it clear you know that square numbers can be written as a product such as 2 × 2, 5 × 5, etc.
8 a	1	75(degrees)	As the triangle is isosceles, the two base angles are the same. 180 − 30 = 150, 150 ÷ 2 = 75
b	1	135(degrees)	There are 360° in the full turn. The total of the angles shown is 45 + 90 + 90 = 225. 360 − 225 = 135
9	3 or 2 or 1	(£)62.50 125 seen 1000 grams seen	This is a Using and Applying maths question. You have to convert 1 kg to grams (1000 grams), then divide 1000 by 8 (= 125). You then have to change 125 fifty pence coins into pounds.

10 a	2	Any three points on line and the corresponding values for $x + 1$	The possible values are: $(-2, -1)$, -1; $(-1, 0)$, 0; $(0, 1)$, 1; $(1, 2)$, 2; $(2, 3)$, 3; $(3, 4)$, 4; $(4, 5)$, 5; $(5, 6)$, 6. You can read the coordinates from the graph.
	or		
	1	Two points and the corresponding values	
b	1	$y = x + 1$	You should see that the second line of the table is equal to the y-value of the coordinate.
c	1	A line parallel to $y = x + 1$ passing through $(0, 3)$	The line is parallel to the given line but passes through 3 on the y-axis rather than 1.
11 a	1	219.8 to 220 (cm)	The formula for the circumference is $C = \pi d$ or $C = 2\pi r$.
b	2	2200–2300	5 kilometres is 5000 metres which is 500 000 cm.
	or		
	1	digits 22 or 23 seen	$500\,000 \div 70\pi = 2273.64$. The answer only has to be approximate, so you can round off.

Mental Mathematics Test Answers

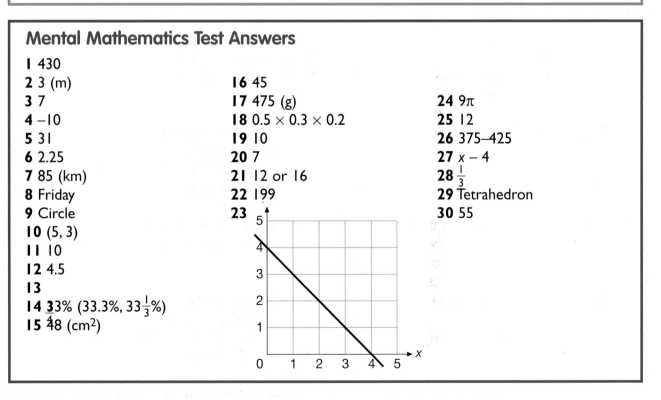

1 430
2 3 (m)
3 7
4 −10
5 31
6 2.25
7 85 (km)
8 Friday
9 Circle
10 (5, 3)
11 10
12 4.5
13
14 33% (33.3%, $33\frac{1}{3}$%)
15 48 (cm²)

16 45
17 475 (g)
18 $0.5 \times 0.3 \times 0.2$
19 10
20 7
21 12 or 16
22 199
23

24 9π
25 12
26 375–425
27 $x - 4$
28 $\frac{1}{3}$
29 Tetrahedron
30 55

To find your level for the Test, add together your marks for Paper 1, Paper 2 and the Mental Mathematics Test to give a total mark.
A total mark from 20 to 44 is Level 4.
A total mark from 45 to 79 is Level 5.
A total mark of 80 or over is Level 6.

Published by Collins
An imprint of HarperCollins*Publishers*
77 – 85 Fulham Palace Road
Hammersmith
London
W6 8JB

Browse the complete Collins catalogue at
www.collinseducation.com

10 9 8 7 6 5 4 3 2 1

ISBN 0 00 719463 3

The enclosed CD-ROM will run on **PC** and
Macintosh computers that meet (or exceed)
the following specifications:

For PCs: Intel Pentium III 550 MHz (or equivalent)
processor, Microsoft® Windows
98SE/Me/2000/XP, 64Mb RAM, 16-bit color
monitor capable of 1024x768 resolution, CD-
ROM drive.

For Macintosh: Power PC, MacOS 9.1, 64Mb
RAM, 16-bit color monitor capable of 1024x768
resolution; CD-ROM drive.

British Library Cataloguing in Publication Data
A Catalogue record for this publication is available from the
British Library

Edited by Margaret Shepherd
CD-ROM development by Ros Davies and Joanne Hunt
Book design by Sally Boothroyd
Illustrated by Jerry Fowler and Tim Hutchinson
Index compiled by Joan Dearnley
Printed and bound by Printing Express Ltd, Hong Kong

You might also like to visit
www.harpercollins.co.uk
The book lover's website

acute angle 78
addition
  of decimals 18-19
  of negative numbers 24-5
  rules of 14
algebra 48-55
alternate angle 82
angles 78-83
'approximately equal to' 20, 76
area
  of circle 94-5
  and perimeter 92-3
average 100
averages and range 98-105

bar charts 98-9
bias in questionnaires 114-15
'bigger than' (symbol) 12
BODMAS 64-5
box method 16, 17, 21
brackets 64-5

cancelling fractions 28-9, 42
capacity 74, 76, 96-7
chance and probability 116-21
Chinese multiplication 16
chunking 17
circles 94-5
circumference of circle 94-5
coefficients 49
columns for calculations 14-15, 16, 17
common denominator 28, 40-1
common factor 36
comparing distributions 104-5
comparing numbers 12
complete turn 78
congruency 87
continuous data 110-11
coordinates
  in all four quadrants 58-9
  in the first quadrant 56-7
  for graphs 60-3
correlation 112
corresponding angle 82
counting squares 92
cross-multiplication 70-1
cube roots 97
cuboids 90, 91, 96-7

data
  averages and range 98-105
  statistical representation 106-15

decimal fractions 10-11
decimal point 10-11, 18-19
decimals
  adding and subtracting 18-19
  and fractions 30-1
  ordering 12-13
decrease by percentage 32
degree, symbol for 78
denominators 28, 34, 40-1, 42
diameter 94
direct proportion 36-7
directed numbers 22-3, 24-5
distributions 104-5
division
  of decimals 20-1
  of fractions 42-3
  long division 17
  of metric units 74
  rules of 14

elevations 90
enlargements 88-9
equations 48-9
  coordinate grids 60-3
  fractional 70-1
  linear 66-9
  trial and improvement 72-3
equilateral triangle 80
equivalences 30
expressions (algebraic) 48, 52, 53
exterior angle 80

factors 46-7
flow diagrams 50
formulae 50-3
  area and circumference 93, 94-5
four rules 14-15
fractional equations 70-1
fractions
  and percentages 26-31
  and ratios 40-3
frequency diagrams 102-3, 110-11
frequency tables 98-9, 101, 108, 110-11

graphs
  coordinates for 60-3
  line graphs 106-7
greater than (bigger than) 12
grouped data 102-3

hundredths 10

identities (algebraic) 48
image and object 86-7
imperial units 76-7
increase by a percentage 32
independent events 120
input 50, 52-3
interior angle 80, 82
inverse operation 52, 53
  linear equations 66, 67, 68
isometric drawings 91
isosceles triangle 80

kite 85

LCM 40-1
length 74, 76
less than 12
letters, for values 48-9
line of best fit 112, 113
line graphs 106-7
linear equations 66-9
lines of the form 62-3
long division 16, 17
long multiplication 16
lowest common multiple 40-1
lowest term (fractions) 28
mean 100-1, 104, 105
median 100, 104
metric units 74-5
minus signs 24-5
mirror line 86
mode 98, 100, 104
multiples 46-7
multiplication
  of decimals 20-1
  of fractions 42-3
  of metric units 74
multiplication tables 14
multipliers 32-3
mutually exclusive events 116

Napier's bones 16
negative numbers 22-5
nets 90
  and shapes 84-91
nth term 54-5
number line 12
  adding and subtracting decimals 18-19
  negative and positive numbers 24-5
number patterns 44-5
numerators 28, 34, 30-1, 42

object and image 86-7
obtuse angle 78
operations
  algebraic formulae with two operations 52-3
  inverse, for linear equations 66, 67, 68
order (or power) 64
origin
  coordinates in all four quadrants 58-9
  coordinates in the first quadrant 57-8
'out of' 34
output 50, 52-3

parallel lines 82
parallelogram 85
percentages 32-5
  and decimals 30
  and fractions 26-31
perimeter 92-3
pi (π) 94-5
pie charts 26, 27, 108-9
place value 10-11
planes of symmetry 91
plans 90
plus signs 24-5
polygons 83, 90
polyhedra 90-1
positive numbers 22, 24-5
powers
  BODMAS 64
  power 2 46
probability 116-21
proportion
  fractions and percentages 26-7
  and ratio 36-7, 38

quadrants
  coordinates in all four 58-9
  coordinates in the first 57-8
questionnaires 98, 114

radius 94, 95
random sample 115
range 98, 104, 105
ratio
  calculating with 38-9
  and direct proportion 36-7
  using fractions 40-3
ray method (enlargement) 89
rectangle 85, 92
reflections 86-7
reflective symmetry 84

reflex angle 78, 79
relationships (coordinate grids) 60-1
rhombus 85
right angle 78
right-angled triangle 80
rotational symmetry 84-5
rotations 86-7

sample space 120
samples (questionnaires) 114, 115
scale factor 88
scatter diagrams 112-13
sequences 44-5, 54-5
series (number patterns) 44-5
shapes
  and angles 82-3
  area and volume 92-7
  and nets 84-91
shares (ratio calculations) 38
simple fractions 26-7
simplest form 28, 36, 42
solving
  fractional equations 70-1
  linear equations 66-9
square 85
  counting for area 92
  counting for enlargement 89
square numbers 46-7
statistical representation 106-15
statistics 98-9
subtraction
  chunking method 17
  of decimals 18-19
  of negative numbers 24-5
  rules of 14
surveys 98, 114-15
symbols
  for 'approximately equal to' 20, 76
  for 'bigger than' 12
  for degrees 78
  pi (π) 94-5
  square numbers 46
symmetry 84-5
  planes of symmetry 91

tables 14
tally charts 98, 99, 101
tenths 10
term-to-term rule 44, 45
thousandths 12
3-D shapes 90-1, 96-7
top heavy fractions 40, 41
trapezium 85

trial and improvement 72-3
triangle 80
triangle numbers 44
2-D shapes 83, 90

unitary method 36
units 74-7

variables
  coordinate grids 60-1
  fractional equations 70-1
  linear equations 66-9
  scatter diagrams 112
vertex (plural vertices) 89
volume 96-7

weight 74, 76
words in formulae 50-1

x-axis/x-coordinates
  in all four quadrants 58-9
  coordinate grids 60-3
  coordinates in the first quadrant 56-7

y-axis/y-coordinates
  in all four quadrants 58-9
  coordinate grids 60-3
  coordinates in the first quadrant 56-7